Love at the Center

Unitarian Universalist Theologies

Skinner House Books
Boston

 Published by Skinner House Books, 24 Farnsworth St., Boston, MA 02210–1409.

skinnerhouse.org

Printed in the United States

Cover design by Jeenee Lee

print ISBN: 978-1-55896-941-4
eBook ISBN: 978-1-55896-939-1
audio ISBN: 978-1-55896-966-7

5 4 3 2
27 26

Rev. Nancy McDonald Ladd's essay in this book is adapted from her address to the Sestercentennial Celebration of American Universalism, Murray Grove Retreat and Renewal Center (October 2, 2020).

Rev. Rebecca Ann Parker's essay in this book expands upon the "Theological Reflection on Beloved Community" she gave in June 2023 at the installation of Rev. Dr. Sofía Betancourt as Unitarian Universalist Association President.

Lines from "Love Will Guide Us" reprinted with permission of Sally Rogers.

Love at the Center

Contents

Word Cloud created by Joy Berry for the Threshold Conversations project, *What Do We Teach and Learn in This Church?* Sara Lewis, Director of Community and Faith Development at Olympia Unitarian Universalist Congregation in Washington, led this activity, and the answers submitted by people of all ages are represented here.

Preface

Rev. Sofía Betancourt

Unitarian Universalists have long understood ourselves to be bearers of love and justice in the world—those who show up for peace and freedom, who side with love in the face of all that would otherwise diminish our humanity. It is meaningful when a community of people known for diverse and divergent beliefs builds consensus on something this impactful. Love is what we express as our highest value. Every time. Larger than life. Right at the center of our living tradition. Our pressing task now is to ask ourselves and each other how this understanding calls us forward, individually and collectively. We may agree that love is central, but what does that mean to us and what does it require of us?

It is in that spirit that we asked more than two dozen leaders in our movement the question of what it means to put love at the center of our faith.

This beautiful book holds powerful wisdom in response to those important questions. In these pages, you'll find personal testimony to love's power, reminders of the centrality of love throughout the long histories of Universalism and Unitarianism, and theologies of love drawn from many different expressions of Unitarian Universalism—from the natural world to the justice rally; from a loved one's deathbed, to the quiet moment before a worship service begins. A common question that Unitarian Universalists often face is how we can be a religion if we do not lay claim to one clearly delineated theological truth. For our non-creedal tradition, the answer is love. Our inherited theological tradition has long placed its faith in love itself and recently formalized that focus by denominational vote. Given everything our world faces today, having faith in love is no small thing.

As a progressive religious community, Unitarian Universalists hold a humbling expectation to periodically re-evaluate the freely chosen covenant that holds us together. While this work impacts the bylaws that define our governance structures, it also gives life to the values we express in common cause. Unitarian Universalism engaged in that very self-evaluation most recently at our General Assembly in June, 2024, where the immense work of our Article II Study Commission, and the more than 10,000 Unitarian Universalists who answered complex questions about their faithful living, resulted in a new expression of the shared values that ground our living tradition. The outcome, in part, was the collective affirmation of love itself as the value most UUs describe as central to their faith, their living, and to the mission of their congregations. We are a people guided by, and centered in, our engagement with all that love requires.

The love that lives at the center of this faith is very simply the love that abides, as Rev. Barbara Hamilton-Holway often tells us. It is a love that expects nothing less of us than the rebuilding of this struggling world. Sometimes what we know of love and justice pushes us in ways we never expected. And sometimes the need to bear such love into the world is heartbreakingly large. It is in those moments that we most need one another, and most need beloved community. We need reminding and solidarity, connection and care. Our freely made choice to participate in that greater community can slowly renew us and even repair the kinds of grief that have been building for many of us, to restore what we long to hold at our own centers and to heal that which keeps us from being more loving.

We hold a love greater than we know between and among us, born from all that we hold holy. It takes many of us, in community, to insist that a better future is possible, to keep us faithful to our commitments when we err or falter, and to remind us that we are constantly connected to a hope-filled belief in human goodness and capacity for love, even when we feel furthest from that which is larger than our own knowing.

My hope is that this volume will offer us all an invitation to deepen our own expressions and practices of love. May it remind us that our centering in love is not new, but rather a critical core of our inherited theological tradition. When we feel ourselves longing to define love's singular meaning, may we remember the wisdom in these pages. And may they keep us accountable to our freely chosen faith.

1

The Theology of Love Was Never a Monologue

Rev. Nancy McDonald Ladd

Surely many of us know the too-often-preached dictionary definition of the word *theology* that says it arises from the ancient Greek *theo* and *logos*—meaning *god* and *talk*. And so, theology, we say, is *God talk* or *talk about God*. It's the way we speak of and speak with the holy. But how do we carry on this theological conversation as the inheritors of the Unitarian, Universalist, and Unitarian Universalist traditions? What does it mean to us, now, to do this theological God-talk without simply just declaring things across barriers of difference and disagreement? Perhaps most importantly, what does the evolving language and practice of our shared theology call us to in this time, when the world is so full of pain that it feels as if everything we value is on fire?

In my experience, too often among progressive religious people, theology is quickly and incorrectly understood to be a matter of what one does and does not personally and individually believe. "What do you believe?" we ask each other. And "What do Unitarian Universalists believe?" And "What does the person next to me believe?" For at least the latter half of the twentieth century, even among covenanted communities, it seems to me that we have posed these questions in part so that we could conveniently put each other into neatly sorted theological camps of our own devising.

I'll just come right out and say it—especially right now, when the world is in pain, the stakes are so high, and the work of progressive faith is as important as it has ever been. Here it is:

I'm not sure I really care what I personally and individually believe anymore.

Frankly, I'm not sure you should really care what I believe either. This is not to say that belief doesn't matter. Yes, there are beliefs that kill and beliefs that give life—yes, of course. Stay with me.

I want to make a case that maybe we shouldn't spend so much time asking what it is we personally do and do not believe in the deep inner recesses of our own hearts; maybe that highly individualistic and utterly non-relational question "What do you believe?" isn't the point of theology in the first place. After all, theology is a conversation. Remember that old dictum we started with? It's God-talk. Theology is not an inner monologue for the purposes of one's own clarification and edification. It isn't talking to oneself about oneself for oneself. At the very least, theology is a dialogue, and so the question that I think is most pertinent to our history and our time is not so much "What do I believe?" as it is "With whom am I in holy and accountable conversation?"

Perhaps my theology isn't actually about me at all. If love, or relationality, or commitment to interconnection really lies at the center, then theology hasn't ever been about me. It's about who I'm in covenant with, what that covenant asks of me, and how I am held by that covenant in relationship to that force which is and will always be so much larger than myself alone.

This train of thought was galvanized when I ran across an interview from the University of Chicago Divinity School with Dr. Susan Schreiner, who retired not long ago after teaching the history of Christianity and theology for many years. Dr. Schreiner was asked why, in her teaching of the patristic fathers of the early church, she often tells students not to ask questions of their forebears. Instead, she says, students of theology should ask what deep and powerful questions their theological forebears are asking them.

As she so succinctly put it, "Theology is not about you." As such, the first work of theological inquiry, or of textual study, or of history for that matter, is the work of attending, not the work of declaring. In her words, "It takes a lot to realize that you are not the most important person in the world, that *your* questions might not be the right questions or the most profound questions."[1]

It takes a lot to enter into the theological enterprise first as a learner rather than as a declarer-of-stuff or disprover-of-things. If there is one single thing I hope to accomplish in my life as a person who thinks in theological terms, it's to be a listener first of all, instead of a declarer. In order to be a listener, I must naturally posit the existence of someone out there in the wide vastness of the mystery (or across the dining room table or in the pew next to me) to whom I am actually willing to listen.

If theology is a conversation, not a monologue, the question of belief is one we can approach appropriately when and only when we are able to take in the questions that are posed to us by forces outside of ourselves. And so theology is and has always been much more about relationship than it is about belief.

As we often say, *we are a covenantal faith rather than a creedal one.* We speak of how we want to be together rather than a set of common assertions we are supposed to believe together. In this way, we are a people who make promises in relationship to others. As Martin Buber famously put it, human beings are "the promise making, promise breaking, promise renewing creature."[2] The hardest and most important promises

---

[1] "In Conversation: 'Theology is not about you,'" *Criterion* (May 2018). See also Susan Schreiner, *Are You Alone Wise? The Search for Certainty in the Early Modern Era* (Oxford, 2012).

[2] Martin Buber, quoted in John A. Buehrens and Rebecca Ann Parker, *A House for Hope: The Promise of Progressive Religion for the 21st Century* (Beacon, 2011).

are only very occasionally the sort of promises you make to yourself alone. If theology implies the existence of something or someone to attend to, covenant implies the existence of something or someone to make promises to, and the earliest examples of covenant in the historic Hebrew and Christian traditions from which we draw our theological sustenance were definitely not made alone in quiet attic rooms with lots of uninterrupted alone time to ponder the meaning of things.

In the ancient world from which we draw this covenant tradition, a covenant was kind of like a contract or a notarized document. It set out the framework for a relationship, the promises and conditions under which that relationship would proceed. In the Christian tradition, it is commonly understood that the four Hebraic covenants are joined by the fifth and full covenant of the people with God, realized in the death and resurrection of Jesus and carrying with it a promise of salvation. For our Universalist ancestors, this fifth covenant was not a partial covenant, but a complete one. It held within it the promise of salvation for all, mediated through the person of Jesus but fundamentally made by a God whose radical love could not and would not be forsaken, not even by the most obnoxious, stubborn, and even objectively death-dealing of God's people.

In this way, the covenants of our theological ancestors were not merely a set of behavioral ground rules that the people made between each other. Rather, they were promises negotiated, made, and lived out in relationship to a living God. In the case of our Universalist ancestors, this was a living God whose very essence in this world was the experience of irresistible and ever-present love.

During the pandemic, we honored the 250th anniversary of John Murray's landing on the New Jersey shores, where he would preach universal salvation and circuit-ride his way to becoming the so-named father of American Universalism.

Honoring those 250 years of Universalist history while engaging in the study process leading up to the Article II proposal, I thought it would be worthwhile to ponder just who it was this forebear of ours made promises to, and just what sort of God was busy making promises to him. Whom was early American Universalist theology a dialogue with?

The answer is unequivocal. It was God, characterized by expansive and demanding love, whom Murray understood to be in command of the winds and the waves. It was God, or his understanding of God's love, that held him to these shores. In this narrative, it was also God who compelled Thomas Potter to lay one stone atop the other and build a sanctuary to house the gospel of all-embracing love.

This sort of theologically grounded Universalism was sometimes called "The Gospel of God's Success," and it was so fundamentally *not about us* that Rev. Gordon McKeeman later characterized it this way: "The image was that the last unrepentant sinner would be dragged kicking and screaming into heaven, unable, at last, to resist the power and love of the Almighty."[3]

Yes there were those (the Arminians) who mitigated this idea of God's all-powerful and irresistible grace with the idea that we human beings had enough independent agency and freedom to openly rebel against God's grace—but not John Murray. And not that other luminary of Universalist theology we would be remiss if we overlooked, Hosea Ballou. As he put it in *A Treatise on Atonement*:

> There is nothing in heaven above, nor in the earth beneath, that can do away sin, but love, and we have reason to be eternally thankful that love is stronger than death, that many waters cannot

[3] Gordon B. McKeeman, "The Persistence of Universalism," address at the New York State Convention of Universalists (1980), nyscu.org/Publications/Universalist_Heritage.pdf.

> quench it, nor the floods drown it; that it has the power to remove the moral maladies of mankind, and make us free from the law of sin and death, to reconcile us to God, and to wash us pure in the blood of life, of the everlasting covenant. O love, thou great Physician of souls, what a work hast thou undertaken!"[4]

In this fundamentally relational Universalist theology, this covenant of promises between God and God's people, everything we do, both for the good and the bad, is finite and limited, but everything God does is infinite and complete. This is the very thing that differentiates us from the divine and that necessitates God's unending and all-encompassing grace.

Before you get nervous, I'm not about to say that everybody ought to believe in God. Remember, I don't even think I really care what I or you or any of us believe on an individual basis right about now. What I'm trying to do is to make an argument that our Unitarian Universalist faith and history invite us to make promises with something other than our ourselves, in this case a commanding and irresistible force of love that will not let us go.

For Murray, and especially for Ballou, our theology never was about us. It was always about God. And the central assertion at the core of historic Universalism had nothing whatever to do with the inherent benevolence, goodness, or blessedness of human nature, but rather the benevolence of God's nature and the utter necessity of grace to act upon we flawed human beings as transformed recipients of that unearned expansive grace—each and every time, without fail. Functioning not laterally, but vertically, the Universalist God's love uplifts us, drawing us always closer to God's own self.

---

[4] Quoted in Dan McKanan, et al., *A Documentary History of Unitarian Universalism*, Vol. 1 (Skinner House, 2017).

It was theologian Jurgen Moltmann who popularized the framework of a vertical and a horizontal dimension to faith. The vertical is that which transcends us, that which pulls us up to an object of reverence. The horizontal is the dimension of faith lived out right here—among us and within us, a this-worldly faith that calls us to attention and action in this present moment.

Moltmann said that these two aspects of faith, the vertical and the horizontal, are not alternatives in competition with each other. Instead, they exist in essential and dynamic tension, with the vertical always putting pressure on the horizontal. This means that the transcendent in which we are in covenantal relationship always exerts some kind of transformational pressure on this world and each of us within it.

And that, not a call to theism as such, is at the heart of my contention here. It is merely this, that theology, covenant, and the love that will not let us go—none of it—is really about us uniquely and specifically. It really isn't about you at all. Or me. When we unseat the vertical dimension entirely and cease to pursue a relationship with the holy separate and beyond our own understanding, *a thing that happens* is that we tend to try to put ourselves in God's place. Likewise, when we mistakenly believe that theology is all about what we do and do not personally believe, we tend to discount the inherently relational and covenantal dimensions of theology itself, turning it into a monologue of our own assertions instead of a dialogue with the beloved.

When we put ourselves in God's place, another thing that happens is that we get an awfully high opinion of our own personal perspectives and our own inherent individual goodness. We can also exert a great deal of our personal energy asserting the truth of that individual rightness and personal goodness to each other and defending ourselves against anyone who would claim otherwise. In this way, making a good account of oneself can become the people's singular preoccupation, usually at the expense of the community-building mission we claim to collectively share. As one pair of community leaders recently put it, goodness itself "is a designation one seeks to defend rather than something we seek to generate in the world in concert with other people."[5]

Love, however, only exists in relationship to the beloved. Like theology, it is an inherently relational enterprise. It does not require individual retrenchment into a place of defensiveness and self-protection. It does not care what you believe. Love cares how we can generate life-giving hope in concert with those around us. As we have practiced it in our theological tradition, love is not now and never has been something that happens in isolation, separate from the sacred push-and-pull of relationship with each other and with the holy. Love does not happen all alone. Like theology, it has never been a monologue. It unfolds, together, in places far beyond the entrenched positions of what each of us does and does not believe. It is not mine or yours—but ours.

[5] Kelly Hayes and Mariame Kaba, "How Much Discomfort is the Whole World Worth?," *Boston Review* (September 6, 2023).

2

Something Wild, Something New, Something Beautiful

Rev. Juniper Meadows

While attending Meadville Lombard Theological School, my cohort was invited to share in a word cloud what we believed constituted the heart of Unitarian Universalism. As we tapped in words on our phones, an algorithm would sort the submissions and display each word in various sizes on a shared screen. Justice. Kindness. Peace. These and many others had a place on the page, but dominating the center, seared into my mind, was this one word: Love. It almost seems obvious; of course we Unitarian Universalists place great spiritual and ethical emphasis on Love. The word echoes through our sanctuaries on Sunday mornings, whether in song, sermon, or in the much beloved covenant by James Villa Blake which aptly begins, "Love is the spirit of this church." This begs the question, what do we mean by this Love? To find the answer, perhaps we must begin by laying out what has become of the concept of Love in the twenty-first century here in the United States.

While other languages may carry various terms to define the particulates of Love, here in the English-speaking West, we have just the one word, a word that has been pecked at by the vultures of culture for as long as folks have had a longing in their hearts, change in their pockets, and a desire for connection. In these cultures of consumerism that dominate the day, Love may seem cheapened like the cardboard of a Hallmark card, all beet-red, bleeding hearts and candy-coated sentimentality. Even as it is commodified and made for sale, Love feels scarce;

as if we are thirsty in a rainstorm. We swipe left and right in a pandemic of loneliness, too often estranged from one another, too often groping for something that approximates Love, lest we be undone by the demands of the day and the manifold demons that dance on our backs. We want it desperately, but we don't seem to have a clear grasp on what it actually is that we want. Perhaps what we want is to belong somewhere, to something. We long to let go and be held by something bigger: a relationship, a community, an ultimate truth.

When we Unitarian Universalists speak of Love as Unitarian Universalists, is this the kind of Love we mean? In part, yes. Yes, because this anxious approach to Love is deeply human, and insofar as we are a faith of human beings, we must be honest with ourselves about the breadth and scope of a concept as vast as Love—even, perhaps especially, regarding our anxieties about the concept. As that luminary of kindness and exemplar of ministry Rev. Fred Rogers once stated, "Everything human is mentionable, and everything mentionable is manageable." We must claim this side of Love as well, the messy side scarred in bar codes and banality, but we must not be satisfied with this articulation alone. We must seek, and if possible name, a higher Love. A deeper Love. Fortunately, we are not short on sources of inspiration to draw from, particularly as we remain a faith that draws from a vast trove of poetry, myth, and story.

In the realm of mystics, Love emerges time and again as a common theme, but perhaps none so more than in the work of the Christian mystic and poet Hadewijch of Antwerp. We know next to nothing of her life save that she was a member of a Beguine order, a lay religious sect of women who freely took vows unto themselves to live a life of kindness, charity, and piety while remaining free to leave the movement as they desired. Despite our lack of clarity regarding the particulars of her life, by sheer luck we have access to her writings in full, a comprehensive, systematic theology conveyed through epistles and poetry that express a prophetic vision of Love, in all its sweetness and suffering, as the ground of being.

Hadewijch draws a syllogism from John 4:8, with its description of God as both Love and the Ground of Being to identify Love itself as the ground of being, the foundational ontological register upon which reality both hinges and is experienced. In Hadewijch's systematic mysticism, Love is not only at the center; it is all that there is. Love can be the only response to Love. This is not a philosophy of perfect understanding, but of perfect gratitude for the interrelatedness of all things, undergirded by the divine mystery of Love.

For Hadewijch, Love is not a purely saccharine thing, though it is not without sweetness. She articulates the paradoxical nature of Love as both the object of desire and the mechanism of undoing. In her poetry, she writes, "All things are too small to hold me, I am so vast. In the infinite I reach for the uncreated. I have touched it. It undoes me, wider than wide. Everything else is too narrow. You know this well, you who are also there." Whereas Love in our times is often the centered desire as the thing that will fix us, for Hadewijch it spells our undoing, and yet remains desirable all the same.

Such is the fundamental paradox of love. Perhaps you have experienced this yourself. What is it but Love that evokes our grief at the passage of a loved one, the anguish in the face of injustice, the sorrow at the degradation of the planet? What is it but Love that wakes our hearts to wonder at the sight of a newborn child, to appreciate a sunrise, to feel gratitude for all that we have been given? Hadewijch's theology mirrors the human heart's capacity for contradiction; our inner landscapes are so often occupied with joys and sorrows, wonders and worries, all at once. When the anxious question arises in our loneliness, when we feel unloved and in our sorrow, we may ask why we seek love at all if it is to hurt so much. Perhaps we seek to consume love in order that we may be consumed in love. We long to belong.

In her systematic theology, Hadewijch identifies seven modes of Love, beginning with Love as an affirmation of the bond between the self and ultimate reality, leading through stages of burning desire, into the tender embrace of love, and lastly into the abyss of love and a recognition that, in this life, any attempts to fully touch that final, ultimate vision of love remain futile, and yet we still crave it. The cycle of seeking, of want, of longing for belonging flows beyond any final or ultimate spiritual ends. Hadewijch names this final mode Hell. While the majority of Unitarian Universalists harbor few strong ideas about Hell as a place of eternal punishment, for Hadewijch this hell is more of a recognition of one's fundamental separateness from Love. The subject-object distinction persists. One remains one's self.

We tend to exalt individuality, both within our broader culture and within our own tradition. This is not wrong per se, but if we lose ourselves in our own individuality, we may find ourselves feeling separate from our neighbor, outside of community. Sometimes this happens for the sake of claiming authenticity, such as when one comes out and is cast out of the community. Other times, we separate ourselves, lost in our own sense of the world, feeling as if we know enough to stop learning, to stop seeking, to stop desiring. We may discount other ways of knowing in preference for our own and, in so doing, put up a block between ourselves and the world, forgetting that it is only in relationship with others that we may be known as individuals in the first place. To be human is to be a social animal. We long to belong, to be known, to be claimed.

One need not hold hard monotheistic views in order to find value in such an expression of Love, or any particular notions of God. What may be of value here for us as Unitarian Universalists is a shift in where we locate the ground of being, a reconsidering of the lens through which we filter our experiences, both mystical and mundane.

We have been and remain a people who place no small amount of value in reason and it's capacities. Reasoning allows us to better know this world, ourselves, and our place within it; it helps us predict the future and delve into the underlying mysteries of the cosmos. Reason allows us to reign in the rowdier aspects of our human condition, tames the wildness in our animal hearts, and yet is not the whole of our human condition; we remain creatures of feeling first. One might even say that we feel this world before we know it. Anything we know, no matter how detached we may believe ourselves to be, must nonetheless be first filtered through the faculty of our senses, these emergent elements of our evolutionary history, an inheritance from our pre-conditional nature as primates, mammals, animals, creatures. The wild critter in us is as central to our being as our rational mind. This wildness, this anguish, this torment. This sweetness, this gentleness, this kindness. This animal that we are, imbued with reason yet no-less anxious of a beast, this remains us. We may name this without denigrating our humanity. There is no shame in being an animal or a human, for we are simply both. It comes with the territory of having, and to at least some extent being, a body.

We are not, though, bodies free from change or locked in some pure or final form. The body changes, carries its dynamisms. Through reason, we can know that our very bones, those hardest parts of what we are, are essentially new at least every ten years. Our body breaks itself down, builds itself back differently. Age wears upon us. Experience changes us. So it is with the body of our faith. This is the livingness of a living tradition, the capacity to change, to become, and to be undone—not into nothing, but into something new.

It is this becoming together in our coming together that marks what Rev. Mark Morrison-Reed named "the central task of the religious community" as an "unveiling of the bonds which bind each to all." If we may understand Love to be a multifaceted experience of both anguish and bliss, perhaps we can extend a hand into the metaphysical engine and brave a guess at what's spinning beneath the hood: relationality. For anything particularly interesting to happen in this cosmos, things must bump into one another; they must touch and be undone in their becoming something new. Hydrogen and oxygen coming together to make water. Sodium and chlorine coming together to make salt. Light and water and heat coming together to make life. People coming together to make more people. People coming together to make more community. In such a recognition, one may find themself at the tail end of a great web of becoming stretching from the primordial cosmos to the present and on into the abyss of the future. We can know via reason that none of this is permanent, that one day our mother Sun will boil away the waters. The brightest minds in our species speculate that the cosmos may one day exhaust all energy in its expanse, withering on until the last black hole gives the last of its hawking radiation to the emptiness. Some suggest that such a cosmos state may mirror the preconditions of cosmic inflation. Perhaps something new will become of the echo of this reality. I cannot say. What I can say though, as a minister and as a mortal creature, is that Love, more than pure sentimentality but actual *Love*, with all of its creative and destructive potentialities, mirrors this reality more than any supposed self-importance that may be bred by a hyper-individualistic mindset. If our faith is to answer the woundedness of our age, let us lean into our most common covenant, which proclaims Love to be at the center of who we are. May we turn to thinkers outside of our tradition who challenge our simple, easy understandings of what love can be. In our inevitable undoings, may we seek a deeper peace together. Name it community. Name it relationality. Name it the Love that is the spirit of all that we are, all that we do, all that we are becoming, even as that very Love calls us back into the crucible of transformation and experience that is this ever-churning cosmos to be made again into something new, something wild, something beautiful.

3

We Call These Things Love

Rev. Adam Robersmith

I am blessed to live out in the woods, where the neighbors I see most often are oaks and hemlocks, deer and bears, lichens and mosses. I wave at my human neighbors when I see them, but (Internet aside) the community that I am most related to while at home is the non-human natural world. From my study window, I see interconnection after interconnection: lichens on the trunks of the oaks, deer nibbling on green shoots, mosses taking back the yard from the grass that does not really belong here. The interplay of sun and soil and water shape the presence of the plants and animals that are my nearest neighbors. Every day, this place teaches me about community and connection; on rare and wonderful days, this place shows me something that changes how I understand the world.

One Sunday, I arrived at church twenty minutes later than I usually do because I just could not tear myself away from the miracle in my front yard any sooner. A family of five black bears—an adult female, two second-year cubs, and two new cubs—were playing king of the mountain on a massive mulch pile waiting to be spread over the garden. The cubs would climb to the top, wrestle, tumble down, and climb right back up again. At one point, the mama bear grabbed one of her cubs, pulled it in close for a hug, and then let it go to play with its siblings. There was no way I was going to leave my house until this was over, not because there were bears in my yard and it was scary, but because there were bears in my yard and it was *sacred.*

Like many of us, I find inspiration, comfort, and profound connection in the life that is beyond my own, in the whole of this amazing existence. Watching a family of bears playing together in my yard on a Sunday morning was worship outside of the sanctuary and it prepared me for worship within the sanctuary as well. My Unitarian Universalism is equally informed by two ways of approaching the world. I am a Universalist: I believe in a love so powerful, so complete, that everything and everyone is held in its all-inclusive embrace. I am also an ecotheologian: I believe that the nature of existence is revealed in our universe and the world of which we are a part.

There is a complexity here, though. I fully believe that love is foundational to reality. I also believe that the human understanding of love—the feelings, the longings, the actions that we name as love—is not something we can presume the rest of life experiences just as we do. I do not know what the bears felt that day, but I saw something that made my heart swell in recognition. So what can the natural world tell us about love? Where is love in our broader ecological existence? How can ecotheology reveal the love at the center of our being?

Trained as a scientist and as a minister, I am guided by the interconnections of life and meaning, biology and religion, ecology and theology. Ecology, like theology, is a study of interconnectedness. Religion is a practice of interconnectedness, a means through which we humans acknowledge, develop, and value our relatedness with each other and that which is larger than ourselves. I have come to understand through science, experience, and religion that there is nothing which exists alone. All things exist in interdependence, interconnection. Even that which appears to be self-contained (a distant star, for example) is embedded in an entanglement of links and bonds that may not easily be individually known, but exist just the same. Relationship is the basis of being.

Many other people have thought about this before me. I have found theological kin in process and relational theologies, even though their language and mine are not the same. C. Robert Mesle explains Bernard Loomer's idea of *relational power*. Relational power is the ability to affect and be affected. The relational nature of existence, then, is a reflection of the Divine. Mesle writes,

> God loves perfectly. So God must be the *supremely related* One, who shares *fully* in the experience of *every* creature, who is at once fully steadfast and fully responsive.[1]

Carter Heyward goes even further to describe God's relational power:

> . . . as in any relation, God is affected by humanity and creation, just as we are affected by God. With us, by us, through us, God lives, God becomes, God changes, God speaks, God acts, God suffers, and God dies in the world.

"Love," writes Heyward, "is the active realization of relation. God is love. Love is God. To god is to love."[2]

Love, in relational and process theologies, is not the warm and mushy feelings of pop music and romantic comedies. Love is what allows the world to exist. It is what holds all things together and makes existence coherent. Love is relationship at its best, a way of being that requires relational power, a power that values and respects that which it connects. This kind of love—relational and divine—is also practical and observable in our world. The profound relatedness of fungal mycelium and tree roots, of intestinal flora and animals, provides mutual benefit and thriving for each. The presence of apex predators can improve the landscape by limiting how prey consume

[1] C. Robert Mesle, *Process Theology: A Basic Introduction* (Chalice, 1993).
[2] Carter Heyward, *The Redemption of God: A Theology of Mutual Relation* (University Press of America, 1982).

plants, so more plants slow erosion, and therefore more water is retained in the soil. This is nothing if not relational.

Ecological balance reveals the value of each interconnected part: the water, the air, the ground; the plants, the animals, the fungi, the microbes. At our best, we participate in these ecologies in a balanced way, too. We give and receive as needed. We use water and food, and ideally, what we return to the earth nourishes it. Our breath sustains the plants and their "breath" sustains us. *Love is the active realization of relation.* This is what the living world reveals to us, and this is what we can use to guide our human activities and meaning-making, too.

My understanding of religious community is centered in a love that must be shared to exist and grow, is powerful through relatedness, and sustains individuals while drawing them into community. I imagine an ecology of love rooted and growing within our congregations and communities, a vast interconnectedness of our own forests and oceans, plains and deserts. The world itself tells us that a system can have space to include a vast diversity of people and ideas that engender life and growth in a myriad of forms. Ecologies tell us that, when healthy, a system can act to preserve its own dynamic balance. They tell us that we who are the ecosystem can identify those things that are damaging or dangerous and either lead them into health or release them to their own fate.

Unitarian Universalism, I believe, can bring such community into being. By organizing through covenants, we affirm that relationship is at the core of our faith, that love is at the center. I have found a religious home here because we are a people of covenant, of relationship. When we are living our faith, we use our relational power to grow in a love that values and respects everything it connects.

Here is another complexity: Love is one of those words that holds so much and yet we use it as though we all know exactly what we each mean. There are as many ways to think about the concept of love as there are people. Some of us think about it as a virtue or an ethic, others as the nature of the Sacred or the core of human relationship, and yet others as an emotion, practice, or choice. We cannot say that trees or bears or other species love as we do. We also cannot guarantee that other humans know love exactly as each of us does, either.

What if we understood emotion as one of our senses, like balance or touch or taste, something that helps us to gather information? Then emotion becomes a way we experience and recognize love—how we perceive relationship—rather than the emotion being love itself. Whether the bears or the trees feel love as we do does not matter: lots of beings have different perceptions. Some animals don't see at all, dogs don't see red, bees see in the ultraviolet range, and mantis shrimp have eyes that see twelve different colors plus differences in polarized light. We do not all need to perceive the same way for something to be real.

What if what we perceive as love is also nurture and mutuality and sustainability and balance embedded in networks of relationship? We can observe how things live. We can find in them altruism, mutual benefit and thriving, the nurture of young, and the support of mates. We observe in other forms of life things that we humans do, too. We call these things love when we do them. Though we do not know how other species understand these behaviors and feelings and motivations, because we observe them in others and ourselves, we can tell that we are not so very different from the rest of life. We are not unique in our drives to nurture, to seek mutuality, and to thrive. I do not know what the bears understood to be happening among them, but I recognized in their actions something akin to how I act, how I live. In the family of bears playing, I saw the nurture of young as relation actively realized, and I felt it, perceived it, as love.

Perhaps this is what the natural world can tell us about love: not that other beings feel love as we do, but that we can recognize love as something more than our own feelings. If love is the very best version of relatedness, then love is at the center of Life itself and networked throughout our entire existence.

4

Reflections of a Japanese-Descent UU on Cultural Contexts of "Love"

Rev. Shige Sakurai

Love can be understood in many liberating ways, and yet many harms and even atrocities can be committed in the name of "love." Coercive religious conversions, assimilation, colonization, war, eugenics, cultures of incarceration, discrimination, overwork, burnout, and many other harms have been rationalized under an umbrella of toxic, uncritical notions of "love."

That is why I believe an understanding of a liberating, radical love must be bound up in additional context, values, power analysis, and ongoing community conversations that help to give it further and evolving shape. Love is not necessarily an emotion, though it can be. Love includes faithful adherence to practices that deepen good. Perhaps love *is* faithful covenanting itself, a devotion to live into community and collective values for a greater purpose.

For me, love is awakening to the realities of our interconnectedness, our interdependence, and behaving in ways that thoughtfully recognize these realities. In this sense, I believe love is embedded in the very structures of the universe; our task is to uncover it and return to it, again and again. For me, this way of thinking about love is rooted in my understandings of Shinto and Buddhism.

I came into Unitarian Universalist spaces at a time when I was particularly beginning to deepen my heritage-seeking and grounding in Japanese culture, spirituality, and histories. I was spending more time in reading and practices related to

Buddhism and Shinto, in particular. I was drawn to my local UU congregation because a Buddhist meditation group was meeting there.

As I deepened into UU traditions, I began to read more and more about Japanese and Asian influences and overlaps in Unitarian Universalism. The long history of convergences reminds me that the many and varied spiritualities of my ancestors and the ancestors of my spiritual kin all feed into the modern theological streams and oceans.

One concept in Shinto tradition is that of musubi, a divine and creative power, which can be expressed as creation or procreation and also refers to the ties that bind us, from ancestor to descendant, and from humans to broader nature. Musubi contains concepts of interdependence across both time and space.

In modern Shinto, the universe is typically thought of as inherently harmonious in its natural state, and bad things happen as a result of a sort of spiritual entropy over time, a chaos that departs from natural goodness. Thus, that which is bad is also rooted in a lack of maintenance, a need for clearing and returning to harmony. Shinto rituals often revolve around ritual purification and renewal.

This "purification" is not about moral purity so much as it is about the labors we must engage to return to newness, freshness, clear-heartedness, and the goodness of the universe's natural state. This reminds us that the work is always ongoing; there is not a pinnacle you reach and simply stop. In UU spaces, I witness this as the "living tradition" and as the value of transformation and spiritual development.

Embracing "Love" in Asian-Heritage Spirituality

In the 1995 article "'Love' and the Eastern Spirit: A Philosophic Perspective," Dr. Zijian Ding reviews conceptualizations of love across five Asian religious and philosophical streams of thought.

Ding's article delves into a variety of understandings, including a "humanistic love" in Confucianism that emphasizes "human affairs and 'this life'" and meanings such as "goodness, heartedfulness, or humaneness." The article also discusses "universal love" in Buddhism, as a love that "emphasized religious equality" and does "not approve of special love for particular things." The article further explores "devotional love" in Hinduism as "profoundly inspired by the holy mystery of life" and a "transcendent experience."

Further, a 1993 book by Dr. Arthur Versluis, entitled *American Transcendentalism and Asian Religions*, explains that Transcendentalists were attracted to seeking common concepts across religions. These interests included Confucianism, Zoroastrianism, Islam, Hinduism, Buddhism, and Taoism, among others.

Versluis demonstrates that Asian religions had a significant impact on Transcendentalism and particularly points to Rev. Ralph Waldo Emerson and Henry David Thoreau as among those who were most interested and studied in Asian religions, and who were incorporating Asian thought into their writings.

Ideas about multiple religions and their importance, including Asian spiritual thought, have deep roots and connections in Unitarian and Universalist histories. Even before the founding of the American Unitarian Association in 1825, there were Unitarian congregations in Asia and Asian-descent people in U.S. Unitarian congregations.

The first publication of Buddhist writings in English was in the Transcendentalist publication *The Dial* in 1844. Fragments of the Lotus Sutra, believed to have been translated by Elizabeth Peabody Palmer, appeared in the publication that year. The lotus flower itself is a symbol of the pristine and good arising from that which may be murky or muddied, representing enlightenment. For me, it is also a great way to conceptualize a liberating love. The Lotus Sutra fragment in *The Dial* discusses the Buddhist teaching known as the "one vehicle" or the "one path," and reminds us that multiple teachings and paths are connected, that ultimately we are led toward the same destination of enlightenment, completion, or salvation. Sound familiar?

In this, I read a certain version of Universalism about an ultimate destination, though I am also receiving in it messages about interrelatedness, religious pluralism, and equity in access to spiritual growth. In other words, I am noticing many of the same themes emergent in Universalist thought overall. And it makes sense to me that all of these can be part of the spokes in the wheel of love.

By the 1870s, a variety of Asian religious texts were spreading in liberal religious pulpits in the United States. And the Japanese Unitarian movement was underway in the 1880s and opened Unity Temple in Tokyo in 1894. The space became fertile ground for socialist and labor union organizing—understanding justice, equity, and transformation as core components of what it meant to be a Japanese Unitarian.

The Universalist mission in Japan began in 1890 and included service-oriented projects, such as a home for Japanese girls who were economically or socially oppressed. In a 2002 presentation to the Unitarian Universalists of Sterling, Virginia, UU minister and professor Rev. David Bumbaugh shared,

> Universalists, who were accustomed to proclaiming a gospel centered upon correcting the teachings of the Christian church regarding eternal punishment, found themselves dealing with a population not tainted by that particular error. The Japanese had no attachment to the doctrine of hellfire and damnation. While the Japan mission had minimal impact upon Japanese society as a whole, it did impact Universalism in the United States. It forced Universalists to confront the question of whether Universalism

> had any mission beyond that of correcting the false teachings of other Christians. And if so, what might be the content of that mission, the peculiar message of Universalism?

According to Bumbaugh, the peculiar mission of Universalism was the social gospel of "ameliorating the suffering of others and calling institutions and governments to enact the churches' moral vision in a reformed, renewed, and just economic and social order." Here, we again understand justice as a core value, and also generosity and service, as central to an identity situated in the loving embrace of Universalism.

Advancing Love Together

The ideas Unitarian Universalists are embracing in this moment—around spiritual diversity, interconnection, social betterment, and sharing resources and community—also have roots outside of Christianity. They can all be part of our broad understanding of manifestations of "love."

For many of us who are joining UU communities, while we certainly want to learn and be part of UU traditions, we also want to bring our own traditions and spiritual heritages to Unitarian Universalism. This is not new; Unitarian Universalism is shaped by centuries of various cultural influences. A loving community is also a learning community, one that can thoughtfully consider and expand its ideas about "love" itself in ways that promote multicultural empowerment and flourishing.

5

Beloved Community Is Love at the Center

Rev. Susan Frederick-Gray

I was around six years old when I became desperately curious about the bigger questions in life. I remember how I would lie awake at night wondering about the universe, the meaning of life, what happens after we die, and whether or not there is a God.

One night as my mom was tucking me in to bed, I asked her, "Mom, do you believe in God?" Growing up a Unitarian Universalist, I learned about wonder and nature and how to be caring and respectful, but God was not a topic that came up much, especially at home. As my mom pulled the covers up to tuck me in, she took a moment to think about the question. Then she shared with me, honestly, that she didn't believe in God but if she did, the God she believed in would be love.

Her words stayed with me. I suspect she knew she was quoting a Bible passage, especially as she had been raised a Christian, but I didn't know this. I just took in the profound power of the image her words gave me: God is Love.

This image became an early foundation for my moral and theological development. One of the most powerful things her answer did was to invite me to expand my questions, and with them my theological imagination. It invited me to consider something other than God at the center of religion, and even religion without God. This is heresy in many traditions, but for me, it created an expansive way of approaching religion and theology that is truly reflective of Unitarian Universalism.

As I grew older, the centrality of love to my moral understanding deepened, as did my theological understanding of what is meant by this love.

There are two aspects of the nature of love that are especially important when we consider love as at the center of our tradition as Unitarian Universalists. The first is the fact that love implies relationship and the second is that love is expansive and active, both noun and verb.

Let's start with relationship. Love is never just singular. It always signifies a relationship, a feeling or quality between a person and something else. It can describe how we feel toward a partner, our children, our family, our religious community. It can also signify how we feel in moments of joy and pleasure, like when the sun warms our shoulders, or the sunset takes our breath away. We can love the first snow of winter, the beauty of spring flowers, or the smell and feel of fresh dirt when we are preparing our gardens. Love describes something that exists in between, it is the language of connection, whether that connection is to others, to the natural world, or to existence itself.

As Unitarian Universalists, relationship is more than just important to us. Many of our seven Principles described the values we hope define human relationships: compassion and justice, democracy and peace, respect and acceptance. And one of the things that most often draws us together is not any one shared belief, but a desire for community. Not just any community, but a caring community that enriches our lives, holds us in times of need, and helps us make a difference in the world. A community that reminds us who we are and encourages what is good and true in us and in humanity. Another word for this is Beloved Community, a community with love at the center.

One of the clearest and most compelling definitions of the beloved community comes from Rev. Dr. Martin Luther King, Jr. King described the Beloved Community as one animated by an overflowing love and care for all people, a community that seeks the fullest unfolding of each human personality, as well as a community that cannot tolerate conditions of poverty, racism, and discrimination because of the ways these inhibit the full development of humanity.

This concept of love as universal—not just personal between people or within a family or group, but as a desire for the welfare of each and every person—is a reflection of the theology of our Universalist forebears. The belief in universal salvation meant that no one was ever cast outside of God's love. God's unconditional love for all of humanity inspired the religious imagination of Rev. Hosea Ballou, who was one of the most influential ministers to articulate and shape our Universalist theology. Ballou spoke of God's desire for humanity's happiness and joy and for a society that would nurture in its conditions the quality of love and care that God has for all people.

This Universalist theology, with love at the center, still animates our tradition. But other sources have also come to shape our tradition in similar ways. In the 1980s with the advent of the Seven Principles, interdependence became another core value, rooted in the ways that the teachings of science and a reverence for the natural world inform our faith. But for Unitarian Universalists, interdependence is more than just a value or principle. It is an existential understanding of humanity and our relationship to the world and creation. In other words, it is not just a belief, but an undeniable quality of our existence.

The most profound global trauma of the last generation, the COVID-19 pandemic, brought this home all too clearly. We witnessed the ways our lives and our well-being are indelibly linked to our neighbors, how our choices profoundly impact others, how our social systems and practices could serve to help or harm others.

The tragedy of the pandemic continues to reverberate through families, communities, and our global world. And it raises a profound moral question. If, as we know, our lives our fundamentally interconnected, woven in a web of interdependence with all life, what do we want the quality and conditions of these bonds to be? What are the values, qualities, and conditions that should define our interconnectedness? They can be based on profit, power, and exploitation, or they can be fueled by a commitment to equity and compassion.

For Unitarian Universalists, the questions that have shaped our tradition for hundreds of years are about what values should define our relationships. This is because UU theology and practice is rooted in the here and now, concerned with the conditions for all people in this life (not in an afterlife). And for us, whether we have used the language of Principles, values, confessions, beliefs, affirmations (it has changed over the hundreds of years), what hasn't changed is the impetus to have the bonds of relationship be ones that embody love and justice.

When I asked my mom if she believed in God, rather than just saying no, she changed the way I thought about one of the most central theological questions. To answer, "If I were to believe in God, I would believe that God is love" changes the very nature of the question. To have a deity at the center makes the core question one of belief. To have Love at the center invites the deeper question "How are we to live?" because love is a verb and a way of being in relationship.

Unitarian Universalism is an active faith. To outsiders, we are most known for our justice and advocacy work in our communities. This is something to be proud of and to continue. May we always be a justice-seeking, justice-making people.

At the same time, there are those who mistakenly believe that justice is the heart of our faith. What is so powerful about the new proposed language for Article II of our bylaws, and its articulation of the centrality of Love, is that it begins to point to the deeper "why" behind our justice work. Justice is not the heart of our faith. It is the outward manifestation of our belief in the fundamental interdependence of all life and the moral and faithful call to have these bonds of interconnection be woven in love. In other words, we work for justice because we center love in our religious lives.

Growing up a Unitarian Universalist in the 1980s, before I ever knew anything about the Seven Principles, I found a little red wallet card in the visitor's section of my congregation titled "What do Unitarian Universalists Believe?" The statement, written by Rev. David O. Rankin, listed ten statements attempting to encapsulate our UU values and beliefs. I carried that wallet card with me for decades. It described eloquently what I believed as a Unitarian Universalist. One statement so captured my theology that I memorized it by heart. Rankin wrote, "We believe in the motive force of love. The governing principle in human relationships is the principle of love, which always seeks the welfare of others and never seeks to hurt or destroy." *The motive force of love*—I still treasure and return to that imagery and articulation of love holding us together and playing a role in moving our lives and the world forward. Of course, it is not the only force that moves the world, but it is an animating force for our religious lives and values as Unitarian Universalists.

Rankin's treasured words echo in the language that the Article II Commission has drafted for the new proposed Article II to the UUA bylaws "Love is the power that holds us together and is at the center of our shared values. We are accountable to one another for doing the work of living our shared values through the spiritual discipline of Love."

This concept of love is not just emotional or sentimental. And it is not a mere abstraction. It is a form of love that both inspires and requires action. It burns like the fire at the center of our chalice. It's fierce in a way that compels us to demand justice in our world, but also fierce in how it calls us to courageous conversations, to radical practices of welcome, compassion, forgiveness, and belonging. It is a love that animates how we care for each other within community, and the courage and commitment we bring to promote our values in the wider world. It is an expression of our faith made real in the world—made real in people's lives. It is also a form of love that requires practice and discipline to continue to live, deepen, and grow.

Living into practices of the Beloved community is not just an intellectual exercise. Fundamentally, it is deeply spiritual work. It requires humility, deep listening, forgiveness, and open-heartedness. And with practice, it helps us live more fully into all the values and covenants our tradition aspires to —values including equity, justice, generosity, interdependence, transformation and covenants of care, respect, learning, and commitment.

I've never forgotten my mom's answer to my question so many years ago. It continues to hold me accountable to my faith and my values. It continues to nurture my spirit, challenge my soul, and fuel my work for justice. And when my own child, at the age of five or six, asked me whether or not there was a God, I shared with him the same answer. I told him that I did not believe in God. But I also told him that what I thought was highest and most profound in life is the power and capacity to love. And so while I did not, myself, believe in God, if I did, I would understand God as Love.

6

Hospice and Hors D'oeuvres

Rev. Nathan Detering

"Can you get a straw for my wine?" Dot asked. "And can you put one of those shrimp on my plate?" she said, pointing with her eyes to the plate of cheeses, crackers, olives, and shrimp cocktail on the table next to her.

"You want cocktail sauce?" I asked, because when someone is in hospice you want to get things right, especially the hors d'oeuvres.

"Well of course!" Dot fired back, as if I had quite possibly asked the most ridiculous question anyone had asked her in her ninety-one years. Dot was dying, but her impatient wit was still in bloom.

"Lovely," she said as I rested the plate on the tray pulled up close to her chest and put the straw into her glass of chilled chardonnay. She leaned forward, took a long sip, and then caught my eyes before sinking her head back into the propped-up pillow.

"So, how are you?"

I've been a parish minister for twenty-two years, the last twenty of them in the same congregation, and I still don't know what to say when someone asks me this question. Honesty is easy when things are going well, but when things aren't, I'm not sure how much to reveal. This is because I was taught to minister from my scars and not my wounds, and Dot has caught me in a vulnerable, unhealed time.

What I wanted to tell her was that until this moment, I was feeling broken down. It was March 2021, and I had spent the last year preaching into my laptop from my bedroom, which was now my office during the day and my pulpit on Sunday mornings. In the early months of lockdown and zoom ministry, it was easier to get hyped-up for the challenge, but the novelty had long ago worn off and now the distance just felt sad. It didn't help that the only thing I did in person were visits like this with Dot—that is, with people preparing to die. I've delivered and received the sermon many times that centers love for this life and this world, but these days that love felt very much on my periphery.

"Well," I said, too tired in the end to pretend, "It's been a bit rough, actually. Zoom is getting old now. I miss the way things were. I miss people. I even miss the receiving line!" This made Dot chuckle because she always skipped the receiving line.

"But I'm really glad to be here and see you. Did you know I came yesterday to see you?"

"Did you? I guess I was really asleep," she said.

"Well, I guess you were!" I replied, not sure how or if to tell her that I had come because the hospice nurse had told me her death was probably imminent. There at the end of her bed, my fingers resting on the footboard, I had even offered what I thought was a final blessing. I had told her on behalf of the congregation and myself how much she was loved. Thinking it was the last time I would see her, I then got in my car and took the long way home, because even after all these years of ministry, I still feel overwhelmed by the tenderness of these final goodbyes.

"But then I woke up today," Dot continued, "and felt a little better. And hungry!"

"I mean, yes! It's amazing! Yesterday when I came I thought—"

"Oh well, yes. Soon. But for today I'm here. Can I have another sip of wine?"

"Here," I said, holding the glass in my hand and bending the straw toward her. "Just checking Dot: It's okay if you have a little wine, right?" And after another sip she gave me a little side-eye that said, *You know I'm in hospice, right?*

The irony of the moment wasn't lost on me. Between the two of us, Dot was definitely the more cheerful one. Love for the simple gifts of life—hors d'oeuvres or the opportunity to wake up another day feeling a little better and hungry!—might have been on my periphery, but for Dot they were everything and maybe even the only thing. As a minister weary from too much distance and too much death, I found myself wanting to bend, just like that straw, toward Dot's perspective.

For the next hour, Dot continued to take occasional sips of wine, more crackers, more shrimp. I had some sips from my own cup, too, but what I was really drinking in was simply the gift of the time. After making sure I had all her instructions for her memorial service, she gently moved the conversation along to what she thought were more important topics: politics, football, the biology department at the beloved college she taught at for many years, and just how good everything tasted. With such a short time left to live, Dot seemed more present, more joyful, more alive than I had felt in months. It's fair to wonder who was ministering to whom in that moment, but sometimes in shared ministry, we get to receive the very thing we hope to give.

I told Dot as much when I left, but simply. "Thank you so much, Dot," I said, my fingers on the footboard, as they had been the day before when I had given my premature blessing, and she smiled with a nod before reaching for a final cracker and one more sip.

Two days later, the hospice nurse called to tell me that Dot had died in the night. "She even had some hors d'oeuvres earlier that evening," said the nurse. "She was joyful; she was at peace."

Learning to love life when life is beautiful and broken is complicated, but there are simple gifts to be had, too. One of them is learning that love can mean embracing the sweetness of living, even when that sweetness seems ordinary and that living is coming to a close. Dot, praise.

7

Digging Graves

Rev. Sam Teitel

In the spring of 2018, I started burying the members of my congregation myself. As a minister, it is my job is to accompany and love these people through the various stages of their lives, so it made sense to me that I should be with their body during its last moments on this Earth, even after they themselves were no longer in it. So now every month or so I go out to the memorial garden behind the church and assist in the burial of the earthly remains of a human being. Sometimes two or three. We usually encourage the families of the deceased not to attend the internment, mostly because there isn't much to see. There's a lot of digging and root breaking and mixing concrete, but nothing the family needs to be there for. Workers from the local cemetery come to dig the hole, and I sit there, holding the toaster-sized box of ashes against my chest and whispering what I hope are comforting and loving words to the person whose body these ashes used to be. Sometimes while I'm doing this, I realize that the person whose ashes I'm talking to didn't believe in any kind of an afterlife and thus didn't believe that they'd be able to hear anything that I'm saying to their remains. But I talk to them anyway, even if all I'm talking to is their memory. When the workers tell me that it's time, I reach down and place the box in the bottom of the grave, and I keep my hand on it for a minute or so. It's a moment of blessing and also an expression of gratitude to the body for the work that it did carrying around the intangible parts of somebody I knew and loved. *You're all done,* I think, *thank you so much.*

I often find myself in awe of what these workers do. Digging holes that deep is difficult physical labor, and in Memphis it is often punishingly hot labor. But it's also spiritual labor. When you dig a grave, even if you've never met the person, you can't help but have some reverence for what you are doing; if you do it enough it really does change you.

I think this is why I've never met a gravedigger I didn't like. Movies tend to portray gravediggers as jaded and grimy, standing around drinking whiskey and smoking cigarettes while they wait for a funeral to end, not really caring about what is happening in front of them. This portrayal is wildly unfair. I am a professional spiritual leader (whatever that means), but every time I meet a professional gravedigger, I understand myself to be in the presence of greatness. To be a gravedigger is to spend every day in the presence of human death, life, love, and suffering, and to study those things more closely than anybody else even really could. I bury a person or two every now and again, but what I do doesn't touch what real gravediggers do. If I were searching for my own theology of love, the first person I would consult wouldn't be a preacher or a professional theologian; it would be a gravedigger.

I sometimes tell the members of the congregation that I serve, "It is my job to love you. That doesn't mean that I don't love you sincerely, but it is my job." And most of the love that I show them takes the form of accompaniment. I am with them shortly after they are born, I am with them when they get dedicated, when they get married, when they get curious, when they get angry, and when they get sober. I am often with them when they die. Perhaps not in the actual moment that they vacate their bodies, but I am with them as often as I can be in the days leading up to it. And I am with their families after they die. My job, during all of these moments of accompaniment, is to tell people that they are loved, that their Gods love them, that their families love them, and that I love them. Then I help families figure out how to continue loving the person they have lost. One of the deepest and most important ways to show your love for a person is to make sure that their earthly remains are taken care of after they no longer need them.

As Unitarian Universalists, we believe in a love that is powerful beyond our comprehension, and in our responsibility to embody the spirit of that love. The revision to Article II of the UUA bylaws states, "Love is the power that holds us together and is at the center of our shared values. We are accountable to one another for doing the work of living our shared values through the spiritual discipline of Love." This work that we are accountable to, what the proposed bylaws call "the work of living our shared values through the spiritual discipline of love," can take many forms. This is one of the few areas of true unity amongst Unitarian Universalists. All Unitarian Universalists believe in the power of love, all Unitarian Universalists have bodies, and all Unitarian Universalists will eventually die and leave our bodies behind. And it is the responsibility of our fellow Unitarian Universalists to embody the power of love by burying, scattering, or otherwise taking responsibility for our bodies after they are no longer needed. As a Unitarian Universalist minister, I have buried people with beliefs all across the faith spectrum, from Atheists to Theists and everything in between, and yet the work of burying these people is, in the end, the same deeply sacred work. It is the same expression of love and faith, under the same hot sun, inside the same Earth. To bury or scatter the remnants of another human being is a radical act of acceptance and love. You are accepting that the loss has happened and that whatever the life after this one ends up being, this person you knew is no longer in their body. And it is an act of love to tell a person that you will take care of what they left behind. That you are willing to do for them what they can no longer do for themself, even though they will never be able to repay you. And to trust that, when it is your turn, somebody will do the same thing for you.

8

Leaning into Interconnectedness

Rev. Sierra-Marie Gerfao

I am a type I diabetic. This is an autoimmune disease. During childhood, my body's immune system attacked the islet cells in my pancreas, rendering them unable to produce insulin. Because I lack a hormone that the body normally produces continuously, even when not eating, I depend on medical interventions to act as my own islet cells, trying to replicate the continuous production of insulin through injected or pumped insulin. Without continuous insulin, people die. Until the early part of the twentieth century, type I diabetes was a fatal diagnosis worldwide—without exception.

There was a frightening period when my wife and I were both unemployed at the same time. We could not afford Continuation of Health Coverage (COBRA) payments. We had neither insurance nor income to pay for my insulin, its delivery systems, and my necessary glucose monitoring, let alone treatments for any of my other medical conditions. In fact, we had neither insurance nor income to pay for visits to my endocrinologist to keep my prescriptions up to date. As someone who had been using an insulin pump when I was employed, I entered my period of unemployment without even a prescription for syringes.

I followed instructions to apply for Medicaid. The state has thirty days to respond to applications. At the very end of the first thirty-day period, I received notice that my application had been denied due to missing documentation. When I called the office to find out what the missing documentation was, I waited five hours on hold before I was able to talk to a human being. The human who answered my call told me that because they were not my caseworker, they could not assist me. I asked them who my caseworker was and if I could please be transferred. They said they did not know who my caseworker was and could not transfer me, but they could put a message into the system.

More than a week later, I had not heard back and called again. After another interminable wait to speak to a human being, I was again told that the person who finally answered my call did not know who my caseworker was. They were able to see in the system a note about the missing documentation, however, and they let me know what I needed to submit along with a new application. My supposedly missing documentation wasn't an item on the list of required documents, so I asked, "Can you tell me if there is anything else I will need that isn't on the list?" They couldn't. I submitted a new application.

At the end of the next thirty-day wait, I received another letter that I was being denied again due to missing documentation. I had not gone into the office to apply because I had read in the department's materials that the best way to apply was by mail. After another series of frustrating phone calls and long wait times, though, I asked a human on the phone directly if I should come in to apply. They told me there wasn't a real mechanism for applying in person, and they made it clear that trying to do so would not lead to any better outcomes. The best I could do was keep sending applications by mail.

This went on in the exact same way for another month or two until I finally got a letter that I had, in fact, been approved.

The relief I felt reading these words faded within seconds as I continued to read. This was before the now gutted Affordable Care Act, but I had not been approved for full coverage Medicaid. Instead, the approval I received was for partial coverage Medicaid for which I would need to make "small monthly payments" of over $850 for myself and my wife! With no income at all! It was like COBRA all over, simply out of reach.

Like most people living with multiple disabilities and chronic illnesses, I have developed tenaciousness and creativity in getting my needs met. I had been using a variety of strategies to get by while waiting for help: manufacturer coupons, less expensive supplies from discount retail pharmacies, begging for supply samples from a doctor I was no longer seeing, reusing supplies meant for one time use, and rationing supplies (using only as much as necessary to keep me alive, but not enough to keep me well). But now I was reminded that these strategies were only going to go so far. They were not a long-term plan for survival, let alone thriving.

I was afraid. I was out of options, and no job had yet manifested.

I made another series of phone calls and finally ended up on the phone with a human being to whom I sobbed, "What should I do?"

The human on the phone suggested I call 211 to get connected to people who might be able to help me. "There might be a program for people in your situation," they said. There weren't programs that could help me, though. There was a program to help people over the age of sixty-five, which I wasn't, and a program for people who were receiving disability benefits, which I wasn't. 211 had nothing else to suggest.

It felt like the state was telling me to go ahead and die.

It felt as if I wasn't worth the trouble of being kept alive, so if I couldn't afford the healthcare I needed to keep myself alive on my own, well, there was nothing they would do. I know that might sound hyperbolic to some, but people die from lack of healthcare all the time.

I tell this story knowing it isn't unique. Many of you have lived versions of it, probably even several times. It's an everyday story.

Had I died, it would have been considered a death related to "medical noncompliance," as I was not following the instructions of the endocrinologist. Nowhere would it have been recorded that I died because I lacked money.

My wife did get a job a short time later, in an hourly position that didn't offer medical benefits. Catching up on our bills from the preceding months of unemployment with her hourly income alone so we could stay housed and put food on our table didn't leave anything for true medical care. The story worked out well in the end only because my wife and I got placed on full coverage, no-cost Medicaid after—in another series of calls—it was discovered that my wife and I had been unintentionally processed separately from our children. Once it was discovered that we had children who qualified for Medicaid, we too were qualified. Phew!

***

There are some Unitarian Universalists who argue that we should not place love at the center of our faith because its meaning is too vague, too disputable, too elusive, perhaps even too complex. I sympathize with the argument. Rev. Emily Detar Birt explains that a faith that centers love is one that can bridge theists and nontheists. Theistic traditions often put G-d at the center, but as G-d is also known as Love, love can be centered for both theists and nontheists alike.

The history of religious traditions that place G-d at the center, however, may give us cause for pause about placing anything at the center of our tradition that can feel elusive. Something that can't be defined can easily be twisted into any shape people wish it to take. Certainly, much damage has been done in the name of G-d claimed for one cause or another.

That said, there is no set of values we can claim, no Principles or Purposes, that do not require us to wrestle with definitions. What is *peace*? What is *justice*? What is *dignity*? What does *responsible* mean? The Principles of the Unitarian Universalist Association as they existed in the Unitarian Universalist Association's bylaws before the 2024 General Assembly left much open to debate, but we still have embraced the clues they offer us about the kind of organization our collective of congregations wants to be.

Now we have a proposal to replace the Principles with values, and love—as a spiritual discipline and liberating, transformative power—at the center. All of the values are defined except for love. Even if we find resonance with the author of First Corinthians in the idea that speaking in the "tongues of men and of angels" without love makes us "a noisy gong or clanging cymbal," it is fair to want to know what is meant by love as we decide whether we are "accountable to one another for doing the work of living our shared values through the spiritual discipline of Love."

Bureaucracy makes an interesting case study because it does its work on behalf of a good (toward a good outcome) that is often associated with love, which is the sharing of resources for the well-being of the community and/or its members. But in my experience, bureaucracy has functioned with the role of love extricated from the desired good. It is but the machine of the desired good, where laws and policy almost algorithmically dictate both process and outcomes.

This is not to say that bureaucracy is without human dimensions. Bureaucracies are human-made systems to achieve human-desired outcomes. They require human participation to function. They function according to human design. Human design is often motivated by human emotion. Just as the design of our current policing and prison system was shaped by white anger as the legal institution of slavery was undermined, Medicaid's design particulars also have been motivated by an array of human emotion—compassion, fear, disdain, disgust, and mistrust.

As I recall the story of seeking medical care through a bureaucracy, the day-to-day frustrations of the bureaucratic system involved a lack of human interaction on several occasions, but there were marks of human participation all over my experience. There was a mark of human interaction both in the mistake that led to my application being accepted for a partial-coverage, pay-to-participate plan as well as in the later discovery of the mistake.

More importantly, there were affectual markers of human interaction. When I was on the phone sobbing, "What should I do?" I was met with sympathy, perhaps even compassion, though the person with whom I spoke either actually was or perceived themself to be powerless to change my plight. I think they offered the suggestion that I call 211 because it was the best form compassion could take in a system constricted such that affectual powers like compassion would not actually impact the function of the process.

It is useful to examine this state system that was designed both to achieve a good associated with love *and* to restrict the influence of affectual powers, including love. This examination offers clues about the shape and meaning of love. What would love as a transformative power have changed in the process? What is the impact of the extrication of love from a system designed to achieve one of the goods associated with love? What does this say about the meaning of love? Engaging questions like this is itself transformative. What we believe impacts what we do, and what we do impacts what we believe. If love is central, then it is useful to repeatedly both act and reflect on love.

* * *

In Jewish text, there are two very different creation stories. One may be best remembered for the words "and G-d said, let there be light." In the Orthodox Jewish Bible, it starts like this: "In the beginning Elohim created hashomayim (the heavens, Himel) and haaretz (the earth). And the earth was tohu vavohu (without form, and void); and darkness was upon the face of the deep. And the Ruach Elohim was hovering upon the face of the waters."[1]

---

[1] The Orthodox Jewish Bible's text in this chapter is from BibleGateway, biblegateway.com.

Once G-d created light, separated it from the darkness, and named both of them, G-d proceeded to create everything from dry land and water, to the creatures of sea and air. G-d saw that the creations were good. Among the creations, God made humankind: "So G-d created humankind in His own tzelem, in the tzelem Elohim (image of G-d) created He him; zachar (male) and nekevah (female) created He them."

There is never, in this story, a solitary human, a singularly gendered, original human. Humankind is an interconnected whole, one body. There's no aloneness in this story. Even the one already interconnected whole of humankind arrives into a world teeming with life. Humankind is part of, not separate from, the larger order of the universe, even as G-d blesses humans with a special role, having dominion over the earth, which environmentalist scholars have taught us has meant to steward and care for it and its creatures.

This story ends on the sixth day of creation. The second story does not begin as if the first never existed. In fact, the second story begins on the seventh day of the first story of creation, when G-d is said to have rested. These stories are meant to be read together. Even so, in this second story we are transported to an earthly landscape on which there are no plants, no herbs, for G-d had not caused it to rain on the earth and there was no adam (man) to till or work the land. "But there went up a mist from ha'aretz [the land] and watered the whole face of the adamah [earth]. And Hashem Elohim formed the adam of the aphar min haadamah [dust], and breathed into his nostrils the nishmat chayyim [soul or breath of life]; and the adam became a nefesh chayyah [living soul]."

G-d planted a garden for adam to care for and eat from, but G-d saw that adam was alone and said it is not good for him to be alone. For this reason, G-d formed from adam's rib a second human, as if we are meant to turn to one another in our aloneness. This is the story, of course, in which the first humans are eventually turned out from the garden.

In a journal article called *The Lonely Man of Faith*, which was eventually published as a book, Rabbi Joseph Soloveitchik argues that these two stories together are about two essential parts of human experience. We are, as Soloveitchik puts it, "majestic" creatures with dignity and part of all of the good interconnected cosmos, never alone and always with purpose and belonging. Yet we are also alienated, toiling creatures, in whom G-d has breathed life but who are now separated from G-d and what is good.[2]

I read these creation stories very differently than Soloveitchik, and I would argue with him on several points, but these two stories of humanity are familiar to me because we have our own versions as Unitarian Universalists. We just don't tell them as stories. Instead, these two stories exist in Unitarian Universalism as fundamental tensions between individualism and interconnectedness in the ideals of liberal religion as they have evolved in our tradition. By placing love at the center, we disrupt the tension by reasserting the first story as the ground on which the second is understood. We're not meant for aloneness, even if our aloneness is part of our human condition. We are meant to turn toward one another, which is a turning back toward the wholeness of creation.

Over the last half-year or so, I have heard several colleagues reference bell hooks' book *All About Love*, and in particular the definition of love that hooks endorses from psychiatrist M. Scott Peck and psychologist Erich Fromm. The definition they offer is that love is a willful extension of "one's self for the purpose of nurturing one's own or another's spiritual growth."[3]

This definition is limited as it depends on the capacity for cognitive willfulness toward a particular purpose, which means it describes a love that may not include all people. As

---

[2] Joseph B Soloveitchik, "The Lonely Man of Faith," *Tradition: A Journal of Orthodox Jewish Thought*, no. 2 (1965). jstor.org.

[3] bell hooks, *All About Love: New Visions*, Vol. 2 (William Morrow, 2018).

a cognitively disabled theologian, I suggest we reject such a definition. Nonetheless, there are resonances in this definition with an alternative definition that I propose:

> Love is leaning into interconnectedness in ways
> that are creative or generative.

This is familiar language for Unitarian Universalists. We have already come to understand that interconnectedness is about the "web of all existence of which we are a part." In a web, the parts affect the whole. The death of someone who cannot afford medical care may be quietly mourned among loved ones, but it is a loss to all. These concepts apply in private and in public. Unitarian Universalists often talk about Cornell West's assertion that "justice is what love looks like in public,"[4] but I appreciate that bell hooks takes this further. She says that justice is an essential part of love, which means it applies between individuals too.

The word choice in my proposed definition is particular. Instead of leaning, we could talk about love as movements toward interconnection, but this might imply that love has a location, and love does not leave us just because of our location. Even when we are most alone, for example, self-love can arise to meet us. Love can take many forms and is available in all locations.

Our neurobiologies, the ways our brains work, are naturally varied. Not everyone has the same desires, for example, for the intimacy we often associate with love. Not everyone experiences love in the same ways. Mutuality is part of interconnectedness, but more narrow. Mutuality is an aspect of interconnectedness arising in interactions between beings. Interconnectedness

---

[4] If you search the Internet using the term "justice is what love looks like in public," and Cornell West's name, you will encounter video and audio recordings of multiple talks in which he has said these words.

is bigger than that. The web does not necessitate that each individual part interact with every other individual part.

This definition of love is inclusive of the child making sounds back and forth with his mother—whether or not there is a cognitive understanding of this exchange—and it is inclusive of the person who remembers that she too is part of the great web of belonging, and by way of that knowing, loves herself through the alienation and fear of leaving an abusive spouse. (Love, by definition, is creative rather than destructive, so there is no room for abuse.) It is even inclusive of a person alone in the wilderness, where interdependence is more evident than ever as the person works with the earth and its creatures toward survival. And it is inclusive of a system that cannot tolerate someone dying simply because they do not have money.

As Unitarian Universalists, we place love at the center because any good in the absence of love can be distorted. Holding ourselves accountable to love ensures our conspiring with life-affirming, life-giving ways in the expression of our values.

9

The Prophet of Love Near You

Rev. Natalie Fenimore

It has been said that *love* is the word most often sung in our hymnal, but the word *love* is not present in the Principles of our faith. This year, our Association is exploring the spiritual discipline of love—and its power in our Unitarian Universalist communities and our individual lives.

Might we find that, to quote bell hooks from her book *All About Love*,

> Awakening to love can happen only as we let go of our obsession with power and domination. Culturally, all spheres of American life—politics, religion, the workplace, domestic households, intimate relations—should and could have as their foundation a love ethic.[1]

As Unitarian Universalists consider the centrality of love in our faith tradition, we might look, as the Sources of our living tradition direct us, to the "words and deeds of prophetic people which challenge us to confront powers and structures of evil with justice, compassion, and the transforming power of love." Prophetic lives are not just ancient lives; they are present among us. We may, at any moment, encounter those who radiate the transforming power of love. We are called to learn from them and to be warmed and strengthened by their light. Let me tell you about such an experience I had.

---

[1] bell hooks, *All About Love: New Visions* (William Morrow & Co., 1999).

In 2017, I attended the Third international UU Women's Convocation in Monterey, California. The convocation was held at the Asilomar Hotel and Conference Grounds. Asilomar is beautiful, located aside the Asilomar State Beach, along the Monterey coastline, on the homeland of the Rumsen Ohlone people, but it is not particularly easy to get to or easy to navigate once you arrive.

It was quite a hike getting to the convocation from my home here on the east coast. The busy early drive to the airport, a flight across the country to San Francisco, a long bus ride to Monterey, and then a cab to Asilomar. Many of the travelers, arriving from across the US and around the world, arrived late and tired. I was one of those late and tired travelers myself.

And then remarkably, after check-in, I found myself in a room next to another such traveler, one of the keynote speakers. Given the closeness of my room to hers, I was recruited to be the unofficial escort for the legendary bell hooks. Over the course of the convocation, I experienced her loving nature.

From the first day of the convocation, Dr. hooks attracted the attention of the conferees. Of course, how often does anyone have an opportunity to be in close quarters with such a renowned social critic, writer, poet, feminist, and activist—a contemporary and colleague of Gloria Steinem and Cornell West.

Despite what were no doubt many intrusive moments, Dr. hooks responded to the attention with remarkable grace and ease.

She warmly welcomed the group of women, mostly young women of color, who came to form a circle around her. Dr. hooks always gave an invitation to community, not just answering questions and imparting wisdom but also asking questions of others. Her manner said, "You, too, have something to offer to me. Tell me about you, about what you know. What you experience. What you feel." Her words were often soft but clear and direct. And she asked those around her what they knew about love.

Dr. bell hooks wrote about forty books for adults and children. She wrote about race, gender, class, education, feminism, and more. The subject of love was seemingly never far from her thoughts. She wrote a "love trilogy": *All About Love: New Visions, Communion: The Female Search for Love, and Salvation: Black People and Love.* But even in her books that did not have *love* in the title, she discussed how the world would be made better if human beings could be in better relationship with one another, if they might know each other's stories, respect each other's experience. Might we learn to love ourselves and one another? Could we be courageous enough to risk being in relationship with one another?

Dr. hooks writes,

> To live our lives based on the principles of a love ethic (showing care, respect, knowledge, integrity, and the will to cooperate), we have to be courageous. Learning how to face our fears is one way to embrace love. Our fear may not go away, but it will not stand in the way. Those of us who have already chosen to embrace a love ethic, allowing it to govern and inform how we think and act, know that when we let our light shine, we draw to us and are drawn to other bearers of light. We are not alone.

Dr. hooks modeled generosity, curiosity, and building multigenerational community for our short gathering at the UU Women's Convocation. She also asked the women surrounding her about their self-love, offering her own experiences about the search for self-love as liberating. In her words, there was "a moment when the maxim 'You can never love anybody if you are unable to love yourself made clear sense.' Do not expect to receive the love from someone else you do not give to yourself." She further explained,

> In an ideal world, we would all learn in childhood to love ourselves. We would grow—secure in our worth and value, spreading love wherever we went, letting our light shine. If we did not learn self-love in our youth, there is still hope. The light of love is always in us, no matter how cold the flame; it is always present, waiting for the spark to ignite, waiting for the heart to awaken and call us back to the first memory of being the life force inside a dark place waiting to be born—waiting to see the light.

For Dr. hooks, studying Black Love was studying liberating love. In her book *Salvation: Black People and Love,* hooks tells the history of the Black Community and its present life as a story of love and lovelessness. The people's struggle is to find and hold on to a love that saves lives and expands the possibility of freedom. That possibility is available to individuals who come to love themselves and are supported in "a shared community of concern and support" such as has been created by many Black people to sustain themselves. When individuals are isolated in their struggles against racism and self-hatred (racism being a form of lovelessness), the pain can be devastating.

I heard a revealing story at Asilomar: when a woman came to sit at a lunch table where Dr. hooks was sitting at a table full of women, she was told that she could not sit at the one empty seat because it was being held for one of their friends. Dr. hooks said to her, "Come, sit down. When her friend comes, we'll bring over another chair." She was manifesting the lessons of Black Love, creating Beloved Community.

Because Dr. hooks was a social critic, believing that love could make a person a change agent, her love extended to speaking truth to power and about power: in the conversations with young and old, pointing out that racism and sexism are present *even* in our Unitarian Universalist communities, even at and by the Convocation itself. She spoke about the reality of her world, where *even* as a success, she was offered fewer opportunities and less compensation than her Black male peers or her White female peers and much, much less than her White male peers.

In the keynote, Dr. hooks insisted that we call what she hopes we will work against clearly by name: imperialism, white supremacy, capitalism, patriarchy—an interconnected system of domination and oppression. She demanded that we struggle to uproot the entire system by fighting against all systems of oppression and not merely one part of the structure—not choosing liberation for one group only but liberating love for all those suffering. I found myself perking up, leaning in to hear every forceful word from this person I had come to know as a gentle soul. Clearly, her love demanded engagement, action. It was powerful love.

At that convocation in Asilomar, Dr. hooks demonstrated how relational and salvific love, as a liberating and communal force, could be at the center of both public and private life.

The love at the center of Unitarian Universalism is also relational. Unitarian Universalist theologies seek to examine the connections between individuals and between communities; they seek to build faithfulness to our commonalities, our best selves, our desires for peace, justice, and freedom. Our theologies are not only studies of God(s) or of religious traditions, but examinations of the divinity within and around us. A theological exploration of love is a commitment to this relational way of being and to the action needed to maintain meaningful and healthy individuals and communities of care. Love is at the core of our Unitarian Universalist covenant, and acting in loving ways is how we show allegiance to this covenant.

We can embody this love in our everyday way of interacting with one another, like the graciousness of Dr. hooks. It can be shown in the demands for justice and equity and a call to reshape our world for the better, as written and spoken by bell hooks and so many other prophetic voices. We can live into the wisdom we find not just in the words and deeds of ancient prophets, but in the presence of those among us now, today and any day. Do you, can you, see the prophets of love around you? Can you follow their example in word and deed? Can you take up the challenge to become a prophet of love yourself?

Dr. bell hooks died in 2021 at age 69, joining the ancestors, many of whom knew her by her family name Gloria Jean Watkins. I continue to reflect on my precious time spent with her prophetic presence, full of the power of liberating love. I can still look across my bedroom and see the purse I bought while shopping with her at a Goodwill store in Monterey, California. I hear her laughing and talking as we go through the racks trying to find a good deal. I hear her telling me that prices are lower at the Goodwill in her Kentucky town.

It was a perfect loving day.

10

Behind the Shade

Glen Thomas Rideout

Oddly enough, he meant it as a compliment. I'm confident he did, though, in truth, I never asked. I don't think I needed to. Grindr's hardly the place for nuanced clarifications. The guy probably figured he was flattering in that twisted way some people do when they think they're clever. After all, who's got time for soul-searching between yet another "You up?" and "You into?" There's a certain efficiency to it, I suppose—cut through the small talk, get right to the slurs. He probably didn't even blink. Neither did I.

You'd think a slur like that might elicit a stronger reaction, but the shock wears off after a while. It's like background noise—annoying, sure, but nothing to lose sleep over. When you've been on the receiving end as often as I have, you start treating it like spambots: delete, move on, forget. The Internet moves too fast for anything else. Adapt, or be overwhelmed. The toll is heavy, but what choice do I have? You learn to take the hits, keep scrolling, and try not to think too hard about what it all says about the world we live in.

But what does it say about us, really, when slurs become just another part of the landscape? When the sting of racism or homophobia is just another ping in a sea of notifications? We've trained ourselves to dismiss the insult, to move on without pausing to feel its weight. Our digital lives, speeding forward without pause, have numbed us to the violence we endure every damn day. And in that numbness, we lose a little more of our humanity.

Grindr didn't create this world; we did. With every swipe, every purchase, every moment spent in the thrall of convenience over connection, we've shown capitalism what our hearts truly value. And capitalism, in its ruthless efficiency, has reflected that back to us, unfiltered, unforgiving. We're left to deal with the fallout: a world where intimacy is measured in pixels and prejudice in profile pics.

Jesus once said that where our money is, so too is our heart. The strategies of these platforms aren't arbitrary; they're designed to cater to our every whim, to make us feel seen and wanted—even if it's by a bot. But in this rush to be connected, we've traded something vital. We've traded depth for convenience, meaning for expedience. And in this exchange, a slur becomes just another notification, easily swiped away. If this is where our hearts lie, what does it say about the state of our souls?

Navigating Grindr feels less like reading a novel and more like flipping through a catalog of isolation—a series of glossy pages filled with curated images that tell you nothing of the real lives behind them. Each profile is a carefully edited version of reality, a mask of bravado hiding a well of loneliness. You might find yourself scrolling past dozens of these polished facades, only to be struck by a sudden, unexpected connection—a momentary flash of authenticity that reminds you of what's missing in the rest.

One night, after the usual parade of profiles and empty exchanges, I found myself in a conversation that didn't begin with "stats?" but with something raw, something real. He was tired—tired of performing, tired of pretending to be someone he wasn't just to fit into a world that barely saw him. We stripped away the façades, speaking deep into the night. In that moment, I realized how starved we are for real connection, how much we yearn to be seen in our full complexity. But why should this be the exception? If our churches can't hold space for this kind of truth, then what are we doing?

So did I bring any of this to my UU church? Did I think I could? Would I even risk it? Not a chance. I laughed at myself for even considering it, and that laugh cut deep. How could I, a leader in this faith, feel so estranged from the very place that should be my refuge? The absurdity of it was like a punch to the gut. My soul was in trouble, and it knew nowhere to go.

Grindr raises a broader question: Is the church prepared to minister to the full spectrum of our lived experiences? Conversations about living in this body, navigating the world in this skin, and experiencing sex and intimacy as real, flesh-and-blood encounters can no longer remain on the periphery. The world isn't waiting for the church to catch up; people are living these real lives right now. Can the church engage with the conversations we're actually having—about sex, about the nature of maleness, about what it means to be Black and a man in a world that often reduces us to the color of our skin? Can the church move beyond skin-deep generalizations to engage with the marrow of our identities?

Every time we open Grindr, we face a grid of faces and bodies, each vying for attention, each one reduced to "stats"—the shorthand for commodifying our identities. We live in a world where our deepest selves hide behind bravado, where carefully curated profiles project confidence but conceal so much of the truth. Conversations lean guarded, driven by immediate attraction rather than genuine connection. The fear of rejection ignites a game of façades, where our real identities stay in the closets we came out of, still themselves crying out to us for their liberation.

It echoes our earliest lessons—how we learned to hide our true selves long before we knew the cost. We learned that society will reward our compliance with what's supposedly normal and punishes deviation, leaving us to reveal only the parts of ourselves we're sure will be accepted. The church, too often, mirrors this. The church too often shies away from the uncomfortable truths and deeper conversations that might well shake the status quo beyond repair.

Can the church reach beyond the surface, beyond the "stats" and bravado, to minister to the deep needs beneath? Can it speak to the sacredness of our sexual lives, the intricacies of our identities, the rawness of our fears and desires? The church has long claimed love as its foundation, but is it ready to love us in our full and inconvenient complexities?

Picture this: a late-night chat on Grindr, one that starts with casual racism but doesn't end there. Instead, it sparks a fire—a group of men of color forming a circle, reclaiming their power, building something deeper, something real. For this transformation to happen, we need a church ready to engage deeply, willing to get its hands dirty with the real, messy parts of our lives.

Our calling is not merely to stand by as a refuge, but to unleash love's power in us as a countercultural force that digs into the real, messy details of life. Fear too often holds us back—fear of the same things that scare the world around us. We avoid what society avoids. The sharp edge of our intentional difference has dulled over the years. Our commitment to spiritual rest has softened. In distancing ourselves from conservatism, we've often swung too far, becoming passive in a world that desperately needs an active, responsive church.

The willingness of the church to engage with the uncomfortable truths of people's real lives is crucial. We often speak of maleness, Blackness, and sex at a theoretical level, but when it comes to the lived experience, we fall short. The uncomfortable truths that should be central to our ministry are too often sidestepped. Real ministry isn't just about making people feel whole; it's about knowing how to stitch people together again, understanding the wounds, and knowing where the stitches are needed.

Jesus' ministry was marked not by distance but by a radical proximity to those whom society had marginalized. In a world that ostracized the sick, the outcast, and the sinner, Jesus moved toward them, not away. He didn't just offer comfort from a distance; he engaged with those deemed untouchable. In the Gospel of Matthew, Jesus reached out and touched the leper, a person isolated by his community. This act wasn't just about physical healing; it was a deliberate challenge to the societal norms that kept people at arm's length, a profound statement that true ministry demands intimacy, understanding, and a willingness to break through the barriers that separate us.

John tells of Jesus' encounter with a man beside the healing pool of Bethesda. He had been sick for thirty-eight years, and his efforts this day could only get him close but not all the way to the waters that could unmake his infirmity. First of all, Jesus stopped and noticed him–that's remarkable enough. Still, what he chose to ask first was stunning, yet so simple we almost forget to hear it: "Where are your people?" And in four words, the prophet renders a deep indictment of a community that had failed to care for one of its own, one that means to shake the status quo even to this day. To see the person in their full humanity, to ask the hard questions about the societal structures that left people abandoned in their suffering, to conjure healing by understanding the wounds that needed healing in the first place—wounds inflicted not just by illness but by the apathy and neglect of those who were supposed to care. This is the ministry. This is the revolution.

We've lost sight of the fact that sometimes, what's needed most is for the church to slow the pace, to really see people as they are, and to revive an ancient faith in the transformative power of love—and insist on stopping everything pretending to be progress until that love drives everything we do.

Welcome is just a word unless our sanctuaries become places where we can lay down our burdens. I need a place to bring the exhaustion of being Black and gay in a world that reduces me to stats and slurs—a place where love isn't just kind but fierce, unyielding. We need worship that doesn't shy away from the hard stuff, that challenges us to confront our prejudices, even when they show up in the pew next to us. Pastoral care isn't just about holding hands and offering prayers—it's about equipping each other to stand in the fire of this world and still find joy, still find love. If we're serious about putting love at the center, then let's act like it: let's get uncomfortable, let's get real, and let's get to work.

Unitarian Universalism holds the potential to be a transformative force. We are intricate tapestries of experiences and identities woven together to form the fabric of our beings. To truly embody love, our faith must embrace these complexities, honor them, and seek to understand the intersections that make us human, that make us whole.

The future isn't waiting. Love demands an answer, now. Will we rise to the challenge, confront our discomfort, and tear down the walls that keep us from living the love we preach?

The world will only embrace a UU church that confronts its inner conflicts, sheds the burdens of its past, and steps up to guide the people of today. We must rise to this occasion. We must be the church that welcomes everyone—the Black gay man on Grindr numbed by slurs, the white gay man grappling with latent racism, and all others yearning for acceptance. We must be the church that love calls us to be, a beacon in the stormy sea of a world that desperately needs it.

Prophetic church, the future is calling. How will we respond? We can no longer wait; the time to act is now.

11

Love Makes a Family

Liz James

I knew I was Unitarian within the first five minutes of my first service. The service leader said, "We welcome you as you are. With your doubts, as well as your convictions. With your hopes, and your fears. Whatever your faith, whatever your heritage, whomever you love . . . . Today you are a part of our religious community".

And I was home.

I dove in to church leadership right away. And I was *great* at it.

I don't mean to brag, but my work on the Care and Connection Committee drew such attention that they promoted me to the role of chair at our second meeting.

Even though I was pretty much *brand new.*

Clearly, I was nailing it.

I was going to fill the shoes of *Pat Adams*, who was stepping down.

Pat Adams wasn't just the head of the Care and Connection Committee. She *was* the Care and Connection Committee. She was a warrior badass love-filled inspirational matriarch person, and I wanted to be just like her someday. I had decided that she would be my mentor.

Which is why I was heartbroken to learn she was dying.

This wasn't news to anyone but me—Pat was in her seventies and had been fighting cancer for more than a decade. This would not, it turned out, be the last round of that fight. But she was drawing closer to the end.

As incoming Chair of the Care and Connection Committee, I was in charge of doing a hospital visit.

I was determined. Pat had cared for everyone who needed it in the congregation for decades, and she deserved every support in the world. For my part, that meant I was going to do the *best death bed visit ever.*

I had done my research. Googling "how to talk to dying people" had not proved particularly fruitful. I asked my fiancé, who worked with cancer patients, for advice as he was dropping me off at the hospital.

He had said that sometimes dying people do want to talk about death, and that it's good to be there just to listen. He also said that it was important to follow Pat's lead.

"I don't know," I said, to that last part. "She asked me to bring the minutes of the Care and Connection meeting she missed. What does that mean?"

Gary laughed.

"I hope you brought them," he said.

Now I stood outside Pat's hospital room, running over potential opening sentences in my mind. Maybe casual and funny—a story about how hard it was to find the room. Or spiritual and calm . . . . Maybe a traditional opening like "How are you?" But with subtle and deep emphasis. Like "How *are* you?"

"Do you want some lunch?" Pat called out to me, interrupting my deliberations. She was peeking around the curtain and waving me in. I stumbled into her room, perched on the visitor's chair, and looked at the meal tray she was pointing to. A lone aluminum can sat on the tray. She sat smirking at it.

"What, uh, is that?" I asked.

"Ensure," she said. Then she wrinkled her nose. "They want me to fatten up. All my life I've been trying to lose weight. Now I've finally dropped a few pounds and they don't like it. So they're feeding me *this.* What kind of idiot tries to fatten someone up with liquid meal replacement? You should ask your cancer doctor fiancé about why they don't serve the patients cheesecake."

"I could run out and get you—" I began to offer, but Pat just laughed.

"I'm not hungry," she said. "Cancer keeps you from feeling hungry sometimes."

I held my eyes carefully still so they wouldn't widen when she said the word *cancer*. I sat back in my chair and carefully relaxed my shoulders. This was the lead-in that I had thought might appear, and I was determined to provide her with a safe space to talk about what was happening to her. I was ready.

"Do you want to talk about death?" I offered, with casual sincerity.

"Not really." She shrugged.

I stared at her blankly. I was not sure how to respond to "not really." I wanted to respect that, of course, but I didn't have other prepared topics. The only two things I could come up with on the fly were:

a) What are all those tubes and needles for, or

b) I like cheesecake, too.

Neither of these seemed like deathbed talk.

I needn't have worried. Like many Unitarian Universalists, Pat was more than capable of holding up her end of a conversation.

"How did the Care and Connection meeting go?" Pat asked.

"We, uh . . . ." I hesitated. "I've never chaired anything before. Things went a bit off topic."

"We do that." She said, laughing. At the time, I thought she meant my congregation, but I would later learn she meant our entire religion.

And, possibly, humanity.

"The trick is in how you set up the agenda," Pat told me. And we were off, with me drinking it all up and completely forgetting to be supportive of Pat's journey into her final good night of the soul.

After we were done with business, Pat wanted to know about me. About how I'd found Unitarian Universalism. About my partner Gary and his work, and if he was the kind of surgical oncologist that had enough pull to get hospital policy changed so they would serve cheesecake instead of Ensure. She wanted to know about the boys—how old they were, what they liked in school, how they were liking church so far. About the wedding dress shopping and the flowers.

"And how are the plans for the ceremony itself going?" she asked eagerly.

I looked down, suddenly embarrassed. Surely, Pat was going to judge us.

Gary, Maureen, and I were in an unusual situation. Maureen and Gary were still married, and we had no plan to change this. Maureen's mental illness had left her permanently institutionalized. I had begun as a nanny to the family years ago, and Gary's and my relationship had become something more. This had happened with Maureen's blessing—she didn't want Gary to be lonely, and I was the stepmother she wanted for her children. But her mental health meant that she was convinced that getting a divorce would mean she would go to hell.

And . . . a divorce would have been a lie. Maureen was still part of the family. We phoned, visited, and kept what connection her health would allow. She didn't live with us, of course. But not being able to live together doesn't make two people not married. Plenty of couples are forced into separate homes by health challenges.

So there would be two wives. It seemed like the only loving option.

"Who's officiating the ceremony?" Pat asked conversationally. I shrank down further. Pat seemed to grow a little taller, and the machine that ticked off her remaining heartbeats seemed to speed up slightly.

"Us," I said.

"Do you *want* to officiate your own ceremony?" she asked, tilting her head to one side. No judgment, just checking.

I didn't.

The whole point of the ceremony was to create a sense of permanency and legitimacy. After years of not being sure if I would disappear from underneath them, the boys needed me to stand up in a white dress and say it, once and for all. You have two mothers, now. And we are a real family. All of us.

We needed to explain to the people we loved that we were a family, too. We needed to take this awkward creature that had been cobbled together out of tragedy and rejected in so many places and make it *real*.

No minister was going to touch that kind of ceremony.

So we would do it ourselves. We would stand up there on our own, humiliatingly aware that there was nobody willing to stand beside us.

"Hand me that phone," Pat answered, as I finished telling her this story. "I will call Tony".

"Who is Tony?" I asked. "Can he . . . uh . . . does he . . . ."

I wasn't sure exactly what to ask. Or how to ask it.

"He does weddings," Pat said happily. "You can meet with him and see if you're interested in what he has to offer."

"Will he? Offer?" I asked in a small voice.

"Love makes a family," Pat said firmly. "That's kind of our thing."

I did sort of know that. I mean, I had seen the rainbow triangle on the church sign. I'd seen the rainbow sticker on the director of religious education's door that said, "Ask me about family values." I just didn't realize that might apply to me.

"But is it allowed? To—," I began again, with growing hope.

"Who could stop us?" Pat asked, grinning widely.

I wasn't sure. Who decided what was heresy in this religion of heretics?

"This is what we do," Pat said, her voice filled with joy and pride as she dialed Tony's number from memory. "This here is the whole point of it all."

As she said this, she waved a hand in my direction in a sweeping gesture, rattling all the needles and tubes. I thought she was gesturing to us and our little ceremony. It would be much later that I would learn how much more she was talking about. All the families. The weird ones and the normal ones and all the ones in between. The ones with or without kids. With or without partners. The ones made out of knitting clubs and the networks of friendships forged in gay bars. It was a hand sweep that gestured not just to families, but to all the ways we connect.

These connections—every last one of them—are the point of it all. All the things that love makes.

That was more than twenty years ago. It would be years before I would learn the word *polyamorous*, which refers to committed relationships with more than two parties. It would be years before I'd begin speaking as an advocate for the rights and acceptance of ethically non-monogamous people. Including those in families like ours, but also other types of non-monogamy and relationship structures.

Because I have had the tremendous privilege of living a life that allows me to be out of the closet, I have gotten to know so many polyamorous Unitarian Universalists. People who are not out publicly feel safe to tell me their stories. I have seen, personally, what the data tell us—that ethically non-monogamous people are present in society in numbers similar to same-sex partnerships. When I speak to any congregation with more than a dozen people, I tell them that statistically, someone in their congregation is likely ethically non-monogamous. Just like with same-sex partnerships many years ago, the fact that most of us are not out of the closet doesn't mean that we are not there.

When Pat and I talked about our commitment ceremony, we used none of this language. I had no statistics to share with her. I didn't even have words to express—as I do now—how my polyamorous identity is deeply interwoven with my Unitarian Universalist one. I think about relationships using the tools that Unitarian Universalism has given me. Intentionality. A willingness to re-examine what you have been taught. Honesty. A focus on consent and respect. Careful attention to the way we are connected and how one person's actions can affect another's. A deep commitment that my life and my relationships should be an expression of my values.

When Pat and I talked about our commitment ceremony, I could not have explained any of this.

I learned it over the following years. As I felt the impact of being loved and accepted for who I am by my faith community. As I watched the impact on my children of having all three of their parents welcomed at church, without qualification.

I wasn't the first to experience this. Elinor, whose children were now grown, told me about how she was told to "Go check out the Unitarians, they'll accept anyone" after her divorce. She did, much to our delight. Same-sex parents, single parents, multigenerational parenting arrangements—I watched over and over again as my church lived out the simple words "Love makes a family."

Pat was not there for all of those years—just for the first one. But as congregational matriarch, she set the tone. Especially for my family. She made it clear that we belonged. She gave our family a blessing.

To be honest, it was not what I had expected. I was in my early twenties when Pat and I met, and I had a lot of preconceptions about how people of her generation might see the world. Pat would have been born in the late thirties or early forties. Same-sex couples, even, would not have been out for most of her lifetime. She would have recently been through the welcoming congregation process, but in those days it didn't include polyamorous families. Had she responded with confusion or disgust, it would have been understandable. If I didn't have language to explain my family, I'm sure Pat didn't, either.

Turns out, though, she had all the language she needed. She had "Love makes a family." The rest, it turns out, you can figure out as you go along.

I was a member of my congregation before this conversation with Pat. I know because my signature is in the little book. There would have been a ceremony where we'd have signed it, and we would have been given a flower and a little book.

I remember none of that stuff.

I truly became a Unitarian Universalist in that moment in that hospital room with Pat lying in that hospital bed, tubes running in and out of her body, acting in a way that I thought was not quite dying-ey enough.

I had yet to learn that people die in all kinds of ways. That, just like with life, it's best not to write someone else's script for them. I had yet to learn that people who are dying are, above all else, people who are still living.

I would get better at understanding that. And in the meantime, Pat was patient, guiding me like a mentor does. Surrounded by charts and doctors, she looked for all the world like a cross between a spaceman, a church lady, and a mob boss.

And that sweep of her hand.

I want to say it was an encircling, a moment of blessing. But it was much more practical and swat-like than that. Like she was directing divine traffic. Holding ground for our tentative, awkward constellation. Unimportant things such as silly rules about how many wives were allowed in a marriage would have to wait—it was our turn to go ahead.

Love makes a family. The point of it all. As central to my new religion as meetings that go off topic.

They had said "whomever you love". And they meant it.

That was the moment I *really* became a Unitarian Universalist.

12

The Transformative Power of Love

Rev. Manish Mishra-Marzetti

> I'm building a wall, every day it's getting higher;
> This time I won't end up another victim of love.
>
> —Erasure

Just a few weeks after passing my ministerial credentialing interview, I was severely depressed. Having recently ended my marriage, I was navigating the unanticipated loss of many decades-old friendships along with it. My grief was intense, and my thoughts went to some pretty bleak places. I found myself struggling with suicidal ideation, and not for the first time. I had professional therapeutic support, but in some ways, that only depressed me further; it felt like the only person who cared about me was someone who was paid to.

There are two things I credit with saving my life during those deeply grief-stricken months. First, a highly talented therapist who knew me well enough to recognize red flags and then knew how to work with me in response. I also credit my Unitarian Universalist seminarian study group peers, the group that helped me prepare for the ministerial credentialing interview.

As my depression spiraled, I skipped out on scheduled meetings of our study group and stopped returning phone calls. My depression brain told me that I didn't have the time, capacity, or energy to deal with relatively newer people in my life, like my study group peers. Depression pushed me into isolation, and the isolation became self-reinforcing, convincing me that no one cared whether I was alive or dead. As days slipped into weeks, my study group peers were the only ones calling me, and it felt like they were calling me *all the time.* It was quite annoying.

***

As echoed in Erasure's lyrics above, I was raised with the message that I should build a protective wall around my heart. Distrust was my norm. I was taught to be ever-vigilant, highly selective about who could get to know the fullness of me. I learned not to love too freely or expect too much so people wouldn't let me down. This worldview found multiple sources of reinforcement in my life.

In today's language and understandings, my mother's family would be considered "internally displaced refugees." They were forced to relocate from what is now Pakistan to India at the time of the subcontinent's independence from British colonial rule in 1947. The pain and suffering of that time has never been fully addressed or healed by the nations or people involved, and so the psychological wounds live on in many families as intergenerational trauma, the effects of which are passed unconsciously from one generation to the next. Trauma reverberated within my maternal lineage, brought alive in deeply held beliefs that society, governments, and most especially non-Hindus should not be trusted.

My parents' traditional Hindu arranged marriage was a deeply unhappy one. The two people most critical to me for modeling love and trust neither loved nor trusted one another. The best I could hope for in my childhood home was *détente* —a peace, of sorts, amidst perpetually high tension. More often, there was open discord, anger, and pain, as my parents' very different needs and expectations of each other repeatedly ignited resentment. I thereby learned, at an impressionable age, that love—as a form of relational commitment and bonding —was unreliable and extended only conditionally, when one's needs, wants, desires, and even whims were being satisfied.

The schools I attended all reinforced the understanding that my peers were my competition and therefore not to be trusted. We were competing for grades, honors, recommendations, scholarships, internships, our teacher's time and attention, and, ultimately, job placements. During my subsequent tenure at the U.S. Department of State as an American diplomat, my U.S. Foreign Service peers and I were in competition with one another for promotion, choice assignments, recommendations, mentorship, and professional recognition. I learned not to show peers or superiors my vulnerabilities or flaws lest they count against me when I sought a desirable assignment or a promotion.

***

As I began my graduate studies at Harvard Divinity School, I was confused. My UU seminary peers were casual and sociable with one another, showing none of the competitive Harvard mindset, which I had been trained to understand and work within. Some of my UU peers were housemates or regularly meeting up for meals and social opportunities. Some were not terribly concerned about grades and were taking their classes pass/fail. All this casualness seemed ill-considered. Weren't these the same classmates that I'd be competing against, just a few years from now, for jobs? Shouldn't they be more guarded and careful? I could not make heads or tails of it, so I quietly held most of my UU peers at a relatively safe distance.

I got to my final year at Harvard convinced, despite well-worn statistics to the contrary, that my marriage had endured the changes and growth of seminary. But I was in an eleven-year partnership that I recognized, on some deeper level, wasn't right for me. It wasn't so much that I had outgrown my marriage; rather seminary provided me the skills, reflective tools, and self-awareness practices that supported my ability to more honestly look at my life and this critical relationship. I loved my then husband. We had just gotten legally married months earlier, when marriage equality became a first-in-the-nation reality in Massachusetts. My marriage was more functional and caring than the arranged marriage of my parents, but there was still distance from what my heart yearned for. Given the recentness of our legal ceremony, it was with significant guilt and shame that I realized we were not right for one another. I asked for a divorce just days before my credentialing interview.

What I didn't bank on in becoming a divorcee was our society's need to blame someone for the "failure" of a marriage. Who screwed up? Who didn't try hard enough? Who "gave up" on the marriage? Despite telling all of our common friends that we wanted them to remain friends with both of us, that is not what happened. I had asked for the divorce. I instigated it. Therefore, I was the one who didn't try hard enough to make the marriage work. I gave up. I was the bad guy. I felt so completely alone.

***

In the throes of depression, it seemed as if my UU study group peers were the only people taking any interest in me. I would delete their phone messages without returning them, but then came the one from a study group peer saying she would just keep calling me over and over again until I returned her call. I was so annoyed that I called back. And when I did, I found a caring ear where I wasn't expecting one. Along with that caring ear came an invitation to meet and spend some time together. Invitations came in from the other study group members as well—to go for a walk, to meet for a meal, to go to a movie, etc. Who was seeing me when and who was seeing me next seemed to be so well coordinated that I began wondering whether my colleagues had put together a pastoral care schedule for me. In any event, maintaining the belief that no one on the planet cared whether I lived or died was no longer possible. I had lost meaningful friendships connected to my marriage . . . but I had these other, newer friends in my life. These Unitarian Universalist colleagues and friends kept me emotionally and spiritually alive. Beyond that, they helped orient me toward the love and care that was actively showing up in my life.

* * *

In any given moment, we might not know the outsized impact our loving presence and care may have. It's very likely that what my seminary colleagues did for me was what they would have done for any friend who was suffering and in pain. What they did not know at the time, what they had no way of knowing, was my larger life journey: family dynamics that modeled and taught distrust, which intersected and combined with educational and professional paradigms that exalted competition and the individual over cooperation and the group. The love and support my peers offered me did more than just see me through the early days of a divorce. They showed me that on the other side of pain and loss—even when family members have misguided or disappointed me, even when long-term friendships have let me down, even when cultural paradigms are flawed or broken—it is still possible to experience the power and meaning of unconditional love.

With time and distance, their generosity put me on the path to re-examining my relationship to trust—trusting other people, trusting myself, trusting groups, trusting the flow of life. My colleagues nudged me into a journey that would eventually help me embody love more generously, open-heartedly, and freely. Their loving kindness thus became an important piece in a larger puzzle of healing and growth. Herein lies the beauty and magic of love: the love that my colleagues showed me did not stop with me. The healing that their loving actions promoted directly supported my growth in becoming a more effective spiritual and pastoral leader. The spirit of generous and unconditional love flowed from them to me, and now flows from me to so many others.

Through our Unitarian Universalist commitment to one another and to community, we tap into love's transformative power: a love that is brought alive through our words and deeds, a love that keeps us at the table with others, a love that nurtures individual and collective learning and growth, a love that doesn't just bind wounds but can even heal distrust that has been borne across generations. The practical embodiment of love transcends theories and ideas about it, and even the warm and fuzzy feeling of love. It is about our lived experience, moment to moment, with one another. It is the ever-present opportunity of being a balm, and not a burr, in the life of others. It is about the healing, growth, and possibility we forge together, in community, from a place of gentleness and mutuality. In this manner, the power of love lies in the assurance that its impact does not stop with any one action or individual; love continues to ripple inward and outward, through and beyond, in the outsized ways of which it alone is capable.

13

There Is a Love Holding Us

Rev. Sheri Prud'homme

Love is central to our religious tradition. We proclaim it to be so when we raise our voices in a rousing rendition of Jason Shelton's "Answering the Call of Love," or show up at demonstrations and protests in a sea of yellow "Side with Love" t-shirts, or begin worship with the affirmation "Love is the doctrine of this church" from L. Griswold Williams in many of our churches. In my work as a minister of religious education, love made its way into the heart of the curricula I created for children and youth. It was central to the chalice lighting my colleague and I wrote for Chalice Camp, our weeklong Unitarian Universalist summer day camp: "We light this chalice, symbol of Unitarian Universalism. May it remind us of the divine spark in all of creation, the power of love to heal what is broken, and to be grateful for life's blessings each day." When we taught children and youth about our early American Universalist heritage, we explained that Universalist theology included the ideas that God was loving and that no one was beyond the bounds of God's love.

When we speak of love today, what do we mean? The new Article II that places love at the center presents our religious tradition with an opportunity to reflect theologically together more deeply about love. Theological reflection is a living process that arises at the intersection of religious tradition and life experience. Such reflection becomes a necessity when one's long-held, traditional beliefs about love, for example, prove to be inadequate in the face of a profoundly difficult life circumstance. Pastoral theologians call such an experience *spiritual impasse* and regard it as important and fertile ground for faith development. During spiritual impasse, one of three things can happen: we can abandon our beliefs, we can hold rigidly to our beliefs but deny our experience, or we can "do theology" and evolve our beliefs. We do this by opening to new discoveries or coming to know more deeply in our own experience what our forebears taught. In my case, that is what happened to my beliefs about love over the course of the past few years.

Given the centrality of ideas about love to my teaching as a religious educator, I had, without entirely being aware of it, always thought of love as something generated within and among living beings. I had understood love as an emotion, an orientation of the heart, or a description of actions and behaviors. A sense of a larger love such as that preached by the Universalists who proclaimed, "God is love" was not part of my experience or theological orientation, even though I knew and taught others about it being a defining aspect of our theological heritage. Some might call this larger love *divine love* or *Spirit*. Teachers and mentors had spoken of it to me, and I had experienced their embodied transmission of what it was like to live knowing this love in their bones. Drawn to it as I was, it remained outside of my experience. Over the course of the past five years, that has changed. Events and circumstances in my life presented me the opportunity to release an understanding of love generated solely from within or among living beings, something that can be known, contained, or described, to one that involves surrender, mystery, and faith in a love beyond any of us. My experience filters through my layered identities as a white, cisgender, lesbian, upper-middle-class mother who currently does not have a disability and who was raised in the Midwest of the United States and now lives on the Pacific Coast. I share my story of this transformation as an invitation to reflect on the movement of love in your own life and to consider the possibility of what it would mean to be held in a larger love.

There is nothing quite like one's child becoming suicidal to bring a parent face to face with the limitations of love between human beings. It had taken me longer perhaps than it should have to reckon with the fact of my teen's suicidal ideation. I knew he was dealing with some challenges with obsessive compulsive disorder (OCD) and anxiety as well as his other mother and I divorcing. But I hadn't taken seriously his passing comments about not wanting to live. It was unfathomable to me that my child could have lost his gratitude for life's blessings so profoundly. When it came time to go from room to room, following directions from the mental health crisis team, to lock up things my teen might potentially use to hurt himself, waves of emotion passed through me—fear, anger, powerlessness, overwhelm, exhaustion. But in retrospect, I understand there was something even bigger going on. Something foundational in my worldview had come undone. I had believed that the love of family and community was sufficient to create the conditions for children to grow and flourish. I knew my teen was well loved. He was held in the embrace of family, a co-housing community, and our Unitarian Universalist church community, where he was seen, known, and loved. My wife and I were separating with intentionality and care for our family and community and with love for our children. It took me a long time to acknowledge the truth that my love in all the ways it manifested was, while somewhat protective, ultimately powerless over the mental health challenges facing my son. Facing the limitations of human love can be disappointing if not devastating. But that was only the first brick pulled out from the foundation of the house I had built on the notion that love can heal what is broken.

In the throes of parenting through my teen's mental health crisis, I also encountered what I now have named the distortions of human love. By this I mean that while underneath some of our behaviors as humans there may be a root of love, by the time it filters up through the layers of our flawed, human complexities it can come out into the world as something that does not resemble love much at all. At times, my love for my son was clouded by fear at the thought of losing him. Sometimes my fear and sense of powerlessness morphed into anger. I wanted more than anything for him to do the things he needed to do to claw his way out of the deep hole of depression, and it brought out a kind of desperation and anger-laced frustration in me when he didn't. While this was also rooted in love, it was not recognizable as such by my son by the time it reached him. I'm not suggesting my love didn't matter. I know that it did. But the inefficacy and distortions of my love were also real. My love and the love of our community on their own could not heal what was broken.

Facing so intimately these limitations and distortions of love, I began to reckon with the wobbly foundations of my prior understandings of love. As my son and I traveled the ensuing years of his struggle with depression—through three months of partial hospitalization, two trips to the emergency room, and more than one intensive outpatient program—I found myself turning increasingly to a sense of love beyond either of us or our family or communities. It is, admittedly, hard to talk about this larger love because words seem close but never quite right. Now I sometimes call it the presence of love inherent in the universe. I have returned to the writings of the Universalists of the nineteenth century and their sense of a love that does not let us go, ever. Emerita professor of theology and former president of Starr King School for the Ministry Rebecca Parker has called it "the great love that holds us all." It was into the arms of this love that I fell awash in grief when I fully accepted the reality that if my child truly wanted to kill himself, I wouldn't be able to stop him. I let myself rest in this love as I traversed the hills and valleys of the complex and ever-changing emotional landscape that is parenting a child in the midst of a significant mental health crisis. And it was to this love that I handed over my child to be held as he wrestled with demons, both inner and outer, and struggled to find the will to take hold of his life and live it. This love does not heal what is broken in the way that I had once imagined, but in my experience, being held in this love allows me a greater capacity to be with life, to be with what actually is, in a way that creates the conditions in which healing is more likely to happen.

Once I experienced this larger love, my theological perspective and spiritual practices began to constellate around this new possibility. It did not diminish the importance of love generated and expressed within and among living beings. Rather, a new dimension opened. Sometimes I experience a larger love flow through human form in open-hearted deep listening, loving touch, wise counsel, and offerings of care and presence from friends and family; in the care of myriad teachers, friends, mental health, and spiritual care professionals who have supported our family; in the gift of music received as both mantra and blessing. At the same time, spiritual practices that I once engaged in out of an abstract sense that they were a good idea became essential and life sustaining. My meditation and movement practices began to include ways to connect with a larger love and to be held by it.

Love comes to me in my morning meditation with an energy that appears in my religious imagination as deeply pink, shimmering, woven with shining gold threads, and the words *warmth*, *love*, and *caress*. Resonant with the assertions of some of the great nineteenth-century Transcendentalist Universalist and Unitarian preachers, I also experience non-human nature as drawing me into communion with this love that they called God. I connect with this expansive love among the redwood, bay laurel, and live oak trees of the Berkeley and Oakland hills where I hike on trails in the open spaces of the regional parks. The parks exist thanks in large part to the religious vision of Unitarians and Universalists of Berkeley and Oakland in the early twentieth century who believed all people needed access to the natural world to know God more fully. I feel connected with this love at the edge of the ocean or along streams and rivers. I reach for it in prayer and in gratitude.

The process theologians of the twentieth and twenty-first centuries also gave depth and some contemporary theological framework for my emerging understanding of a larger love. The process theologians understand God and all of reality as always changing and mutually affecting one another. In this theological worldview, God is not a discrete being, nor does God know any more than the rest of us what will happen next. Instead, the process theologians understand God as the ultimate reality that receives the world, is moved by the world, and holds everything that has happened in an all-encompassing embrace. In response, in every moment, God offers back to the world an unending flow of possibilities for creativity, healing, beauty, and love. A key proponent of process theism, Charles Hartshorne, himself a member of a Unitarian Universalist congregation in his later years, returned repeatedly in his writings to the assertion that "God is love." In a way that is congruent with the insights of more recent philosophy and physics, process theology offered me another way of understanding the idea of a larger love that holds us all.

This love has held me through the pain, messiness, and complexities that have come my way in the sixth decade of my life. It held me through the long nights of my son's struggle with suicidal ideation. It held me when he came out to us as transgender. It held me when the fabric of some of my closest relationships ripped beyond our ability to repair them. It made it more possible to bear witness to my former spouse's nine-month journey with cancer and her transition from life to death, as well as to embrace my new role as my teens' solo mom. I'm not sure how I would have made it through with my soul intact without leaning into and receiving love from a source beyond all naming.

My oldest son eventually found his way out of the grips of the desire not to be alive anymore. It was a spiraling process that dipped back at times into desperation and deep depression woven with both active and passive suicidal ideation. It was a constant spiritual practice to turn him over again and again to a larger love, and to let myself be held by love. There were days when this possibility was out of reach. Then there was the opportunity again and again to return to being with what was, to have compassion for myself and for him, to allow the healing and creative energies of life to move through him on their own time. Eventually, as he gained more stability, check-ins about how active his suicidal ideation was fell away from our daily conversations. He found things about his future to look forward to. He applied to college on his own. He got there this past fall, and he is making his way. None of us knows what the future will hold. Knowing I am held in this greater love has helped me hold on to the moments of joy and pride. It has also helped me have gentleness and compassion with myself when fears arise and when I face doubts from myself and others, including my son, about how well I have loved him. It continues to help me parent him, knowing both of us are held in this love, trusting him to the world, as he moves into his adulthood as a young trans man.

While this is my story, each of us has stories of the movement of love in our lives that have something to teach about love. A thoughtful, embodied theological conversation about love engaged with the real experiences of our lives matters because together we are weaving a contemporary Unitarian Universalist theology of love that we hope will hold us through the hard nights ahead as humankind faces a tough reckoning with the consequences of human made global heating, economic injustices, oppressions of many kinds, and the proliferation of ever more rapid technology and deadly weapons. It matters because if we don't reflect theologically about what we mean by love, we might be tempted to use shallow understandings of love as a kind of yardstick to measure one another as to how well we fit in as Unitarian Universalists. We might fall into patterns of expecting or demanding congregations or pastoral care teams or ministers or parents or siblings or friends or fellow congregants to somehow love perfectly or correctly or in a way that meets the specific needs of some individuals or groups of people to feel loved, which can often be an impossible task. We might also mistakenly convey to families whose loved ones are suffering with mental health crises that they have somehow not loved well enough or fail to counter their fears that it might be so. In my view, this would be a great loss and a major setback to who we are called to be as religious people in the world in this time. There are real limits to human love and loving just as there are great blessings and surprises. We can do our best to love one another and to be a force of love in the world while growing our capacity to be with the messiness, contradictions, disappointments, and paradoxes of living and loving in human communities. It is my hope that our religious communities will become more practiced at offering the kinds of adult faith development and mutual support that will encourage growth in our spiritual lives, including our abilities to experience being held and nourished by love within, among, *and* beyond ourselves.

With thanks to Marcus Liefert, Rebecca Parker, and Katrina Wehrheim for their insights and suggestions throughout the writing of this essay, and to my son for consenting to it being submitted for publication.

14

Unitarian Universalism—One Holy Love for All

Connie Goodbread

> We are held accountable to love, not sin.
>
> —Douglas Zelinski

Our Universalist ancestors believed that God is Love. They believed that God was too good and loving to damn His children. They believed that all people are saved by the grace of a loving God and destined to go to heaven.

Our Unitarian ancestors believed that God is One, not Three. They believed that God is infinitely complex and the human mind too finite to fully grasp that complexity; therefore, no human division of God, such as the Trinity, could be accurate.

In 1961 when those two Christian denominations came together to form our Unitarian Universalist Association, it was said by theologians of the time that this experiment would be the greatest theological discussion of all time. From the beginning, this theological discussion focused on Love, with Unitarian Universalists citing Love as a primary value far more often than other religious groups. Recently, this great theological discussion continued with a focus on our Principles and Purposes and the values we share. We had many opportunities for open and heartfelt dialogue. In discussion after discussion, Love is the value most often identified as the power that moves us forward in our service, in fulfillment of a calling to aid and abet each other to transform as individuals and to transform the world.

***

The Southern Region's Leadership Experience was a five-day immersion for congregational leadership teams, grounded in Unitarian Universalist theology. One of the most transformative exercises was a focused discussion on the transcendent values at the heart of each congregation's mission. The overwhelming majority of leaders named Love as central to the mission of their church.

We would always begin this portion of the Leadership Experience by defining what we meant by *transcendent values.* A transcendent value is an aspirational concept. It is larger than any one individual. It is infinite. It is inspiring, awesome, breathtaking, difficult to practice, complicated, and needed by the world. Love is a great example.

The participants reported that they were moved by this exercise. It changed the way they thought about the mission and how they worked as leaders in their congregations. When leaders understand that their job is to help uphold, amplify, and reflect the values at the heart of the mission, their work becomes clear. Clarity makes leadership a joy.

The UUA bylaws ask us to engage in the same kind of exercise that was so valuable to the leaders at the Southern Region's Leadership Experience. The bylaws ask us to periodically look at our promises, principles, and purposes. As a living tradition, it is vital for us to engage in this kind of exercise. By doing so, we help widen the circle of inclusivity and welcome others into Unitarian Universalism. This engagement asks us to rededicate ourselves to what is at the heart of Unitarian Universalism. It helps us to stay relevant. It helps us to get clear and rededicate ourselves to the dream, to the work, and to one another. During this most recent examination, we overwhelmingly found that we are called to Love. Love is worthy of our dedication. Love is worthy of our work; it is worth living for, amplifying, and sharing.

When we center Love in our communities, the questions leaders might ask themselves are:

- How do we live into Love?
- How do we reflect Love?
- How do we amplify Love?
- To whose glory are we about to do this work?
- Are our decisions made in service of Love?

The Love we are talking about is the Love that is inside of us and all around us. It holds us, supports us, and is greater than us. No one is outside of this one holy Love.

This Love is not sentimental. It is not always soft or comfortable. Because it is the Love that holds us all, there needs to be space for each of us and boundaries around behaviors that are not loving. We are responsible for setting, maintaining, and resetting boundaries. We are responsible for making space for others.

In relationships with Love at the center, we ask for what we need and we pay attention to the needs of others. We each make space for one another. We do not claim more than our share of space. Our needs will not all be the same. They will differ and will change at different stages of our lives.

Unitarian Universalism is a covenantal rather than a creedal faith. Covenant is the first spiritual discipline/practice of Unitarian Universalism. In communities where Love is at the center, this Love is made real by expressing and living out the values we individually hold sacred and naming the values we share. Our agreed upon shared values are at the heart of our congregational Covenant and our Mission.

Pluralism is the second spiritual discipline/practice of Unitarian Universalism. In communities where Love is at the center, we each bring into the community our life experiences. Everyone's reality is accepted as part of the story of the community. This is the practice of pluralism: Many things are true at the same time.

Unitarian Universalism is the practice of Love through covenant and pluralism so that all may have the opportunity to transform. When covenant and pluralism are practiced, transformation is possible.

Our Calling

In communities where Love is at the center, we support one another in our individual transformation so that, as individuals and as communities, we can help to transform the world. This is our calling. James Baldwin wrote, "If love will not swing wide the gates, no other power will or can," and I would agree. In the work I have done with congregations in conflict, I see this play out often. Those who keep their Love alive, reflect it back to others, and keep their hearts and minds open to the possibility of Love, pave the way for positive change.

If we understand that each of us is bound, one to another, in living covenant grounded in Love, we are more likely to come out of conflict, each of us whole and knowing we are loved. There will be less shame and more fearless accountability. We are more likely to acknowledge the reality of another and come to a deeper understanding: *Even when I disagree with you, I Love you and want you to be whole.* If we go into conflict with Love held firmly in our hearts, we weather the storm far better than if there is no Love at the center of our relationship. If we go into a conflict and call ourselves back to the Love that binds us together, we are capable of setting loving boundaries. We are more open to learning the lessons we need to learn so that we do not repeat the same conflicts. We will go deeper into relationship and be changed by the experience. With Love at the center, we might even find that we are less afraid of conflict. We might find that conflict is creative when are not afraid of it and we hold Love close.

I take great comfort in my chosen faith and the discipline it asks me to practice. When I make, break, hold myself accountable to, and rededicate myself to covenant, I am a better person. When I take the time to acknowledge others, to understand their view of the world, and take their experiences into my heart as a part of the human story, I am changed. I know I am never finished but always becoming. I am grateful for the loving patience of others who support my struggle. I take comfort in the grace and forgiveness I receive from others when I make a mistake. I take comfort in the fact that I do not have to do this work alone and that even when things seem impossible, all is possible when Love is at the center.

Yes, I see there is a lot of work to be done—a lot of good work.

My Prayer

May we, in times of despair, find hope.
May we, in times of chaos, find clarity.
May we, in times of hatred, find love.
May we, in times of fear, find joy.

Choosing joy is an act of loving defiance.
Choosing love is an act of loving defiance.
Choosing clarity is an act of loving defiance.
Choosing hope is an act of loving defiance.

May we know the love that holds and surrounds us.
May we know that we are part of that greater love.
May we never succumb to divisions meant to isolate us, oppress us, and leave us hopeless.
May we always draw the circle ever wider.

May it be so.

15

Love Is Abolition Is Earth Justice

Rev. Karen Van Fossan

Of all the mysteries of my culture—like how drivers figure out who turns first at a four-way stop—at last I had found a mystery I could solve. Perched on the carpeted landing, I delighted as my fleet-footed mother approached. "A standing ovation means people loved the show," I declared. "And a standing no-vation means they hated it!"

"Sweetie." Laundry basket on hip, she paused just below me on the stairway. "There's no such thing as a standing no-vation."

But I had been hearing about standing no-vations for all of my five years. (Hadn't I?) You take an ovation, which means *yes*, add a word that means the opposite, and voilà!

Still, my mom was beyond convincing.

A few years later, ever-mystified by human behavior, I found myself at the local Hornsby's, a variety store that my little brother and I adored. It was a modern-day museum of curiosities: record albums, bathing suits, winter scarves, puzzles, crayons, matchbox cars, and . . . candy. One day, out of nowhere, there beside the check-out line, my dad presented me with a nutty candy bar—an absolute rarity in our family. Nuts, sure. Candy bars, almost never.

"You know why I got this for you?" he asked.

Eyes as wide as the Hornsby's sign, I couldn't begin to guess. After all, my dad was part of the very same culture that had flouted the perfectly fine idea of standing no-vations. So what did I know?

I glanced at the crinkly wrapper. "Because it doesn't have preservatives?"

His eyebrows drew together. "I got it because I love you."

Ah ha! Nutty candy bars mean you love your kid, and standing ovations mean you love the show. Got it.

By this point, I was accustomed to love-talk just about every Sunday. The flowery wooden plaque, which had appeared on my wall as if by the hand of You Know Who, said it all: *Love One Another.*

That was my favorite part of church, the love part.

As left-leaning United Methodists, we weren't big on hellfire, damnation, or other eternal punishments—unlike many of the original Methodist circuit riders, who generations ago had blazed into settler communities, only to be followed, when possible, by Universalist circuit riders, who promised (eventual) heaven to all. In our central Illinois context, we rarely discussed universalist theology, let alone the Universalist tradition. Yet our own stated theology went something like this:

God is love.
Love your enemies.
God so loved the world.
The greatest of these is love.
Love your neighbor as yourself.

And so on.

At age nineteen, when I awkwardly left my parents' tradition, the reason, again, was love. As far as I could tell, God just didn't love me that much. I mean, the disciples were male, the angels were male, Jesus was a capital-h He, God was a capital-h He, and Mary (in spite of being called the very mother of God!) had been demoted through diminutive pronouns; not to mention the endless division of labor—at church, at home, at work. If you asked me, God deserved a great, big standing no-vation.

But what about the love part? Really, what about the love part?

Sometimes I could find something like it.

Yet still . . . .

I can't help thinking of a phrase that John Gustav-Wrathall, a historian who is both Latter-day Saint and gay, once said: "You can take the gay boy out of the Mormon church, but you can't take the Mormon church out of the gay boy."

In other words, God was still love to me. Even more, love was still God. True, there weren't a lot of Universalists living in Bismarck, North Dakota, my home by choice and circumstance for years by then. Yet two decades after I'd left the church, the love part kept calling me back.

Having long since joined the Bismarck Unitarian Universalist congregation, I began privately tending my relationship with the God I had left behind. I remembered that nobody—nobody—was outside of God's embrace. I found that I needed this Presence in the same way that I needed air, water, and sustenance. As gravity held me to Earth, Earth held me to God.

After attending seminary, which stunned me as much as anyone else, I began serving as minister of my own UU congregation. As Unitarians, and particularly as Universalists, we were committed to the universal presence of love on our planet. After all, Universalism, like many traditions, depends upon a community, a collective, to practice our deepest values *with*.

From its beginnings, Universalism has been nothing if not practical, rooted in life on Earth. Because God loves everyone, particularly those who have been oppressed, some of the first Universalists on this continent, like Elhanan Winchester and Benjamin Rush, became slavery abolitionists. According to Universalism, God's love is not a final reward for a privileged class in the afterlife. Love is life itself, which means love can always find us—in a loved one's gaze, a chickadee's song, the collective fight for justice.

That is the essence of Universalism. That is the heart of our Unitarian Universalist tradition. Everyone can have a place. Everyone can belong. Everyone can be needed. How handy—and also overwhelming—that this theology, this worldview, might be just what our planet needs today. A commitment to the sacredness of all. A devotion to the interconnectedness among us.

Still, it's not uncommon in the age of global climate change to hear human beings disparaging human beings. The logic goes something like this: *I love the Earth. Human beings harm the Earth. Harming the Earth is unjust. So I can't stand human beings.* It's natural enough.

But what if we are so much a part of the Earth that when we dislike ourselves, we also, essentially, dislike the Earth? What if, when we (kind of) hate ourselves, we (kind of) support the worldview that has led to global climate change in the first place, the one that says we human beings are separate from the planet, separate from other creatures, separate from the circle of life itself? What if, instead, we could love ourselves into wholeness? What if we could love ourselves into genuine justice for all?

Some say it can't be done. Justice is too hard, they say, to be met with this thing called love—which is too soft.

But I have been fortunate to live it.

As Cornel West has said, "Justice is what love looks like in public."

In 2016, when he spoke this phrase at the central fire at Oceti Sakowin Camp, I had never heard a truer word in my life. Of all the world-changing aspects of the Water Protector movement at Standing Rock—from collective actions to communal living to continual prayer—the role of love continues to astound me. From the first night I lay down on the vibrant earth, I could feel the presence of love, palpable and enfleshed. It was as if the elders, whose shared vision had inspired Oceti Sakowin Camp, had gathered spiritual values from around the world and prayed them into being.

The longer I was part of Oceti Sakowin Camp, the more I learned to live by love, to put it into daily practice, in a co-created culture of abolition—where every person, every being, truly matters. As a contemporary movement led by Black women, as well as a longtime worldview held by many Indigenous cultures, abolition is less an ideology and more a way of life.

Broadly stated, abolition is a collection of hopeful practices that foster wholeness and repair, decrease punitive ways of relating, and move cultures away from carceral systems, toward full participation of all people. These carceral systems, which include various kinds of policing—jails, courts, invasive foster-care entities, and more—wreak havoc on the planet and living beings, especially those who are marginalized. For some, abolition means genuine safety for all. For others, it means freedom from the systems that oppress us. In my world, it means that no one, absolutely no one, is beyond the reach of relationship—and thus love.

Abolitionist leaders Mariame Kaba and Andrea L. Ritchie describe abolition in this way:

> The ultimate goal is to reorganize our society to meet material needs and to build and resource community-based safety strategies and infrastructure... meeting basic needs that include housing, health care, access to care for disabled people, childcare, elder care, a basic guaranteed income, and accessible, sustainable, living-wage jobs that enable people to prevent, escape, intervene in, and transform the conditions that make violence possible . . . . Abolition is the sky we are reaching for.[1]

[1] Miriam Kaba and Andrea J. Ritchie, *No More Police: A Case for Abolition* (The New Press, 2022).

Abolition doesn't only mean steadily dismantling punitive systems, which tend to punish difference, pathologize pain, and exacerbate the very traumas and conditions they are said to address. It means reconnecting the broken strands in the collective fabric of life. Taken one by one, each of Kaba and Ritchie's abolitionist goals was realized from August 2016, when Oceti Sakowin Camp began, through February 2017, when the Governor of North Dakota officially evicted us:

Housing. As people came and went, all 100,000+ of us were housed, whether we had arrived with our own tents, tipis, yurts, and RVs, or whether we needed the larger community to provide. Those of us who had been there longer would spread the word, "When you go, please leave your tent if you can; others may need the spot."

Health care. Through the Medic and Healer Tents, we had access to free health care, whether preventative care like massage and acupuncture, or allopathic care like emergency medical intervention. Sometimes, moving from here to there, I would stop by the herbology tent, basking in the presence of sunlit jar after sunlit jar of healing plants. In the tent for allopathic care, I received much-needed care for a bloody kitchen mishap—without the need to pay or even fret about how to do so. The community itself was our insurance.

Inclusion and access to care for disabled people. People with disabilities were central to Camp life and decision-making, with access to general health care, as well as the particular attention of volunteer Camp security, who brought firewood and other supplies to those who needed them most.

Childcare. Well organized and well staffed in a sturdy Army tent, school was free and intercultural. In an adjoining Army tent, the library teemed with books and materials for all ages. Early on, I reveled in staffing the library, pulling one book after another for children with hungry minds.

Elder care. Elders were not only served first at every meal and afforded access to various healing modalities; they were also the spiritual leaders of Camp. The day after law enforcement had unleashed water hoses on Water Protectors outside of Camp, in thirty-below weather no less, some of the younger Water Protectors longed for retribution. Volunteers popped into the kitchen tent, where I was attempting to open an industrial can of tomatoes, and asked if any of us had seen Camp elders; they were needed ASAP, in order to remind the younger folks of the nonviolent commitment of the Water Protector movement, even in the face of such cruelty by the police.

Basic guaranteed income. Because food, housing, health care, socializing, and ride sharing all were free, just living and being at Camp was something like receiving a basic guaranteed income—a basic guaranteed support for life. Our little church in Bismarck served as a pass-through spot for many of these supplies, as well as a transportation hub for people catching rides to and from Camp. Those who needed travel funds, for bus tickets and the like, often had access to these supports as well, as land defenders far and wide had made such resources plentiful.

Accessible, sustainable, living-wage jobs that enable people to prevent, escape, intervene in, and transform the conditions that make violence possible. At Oceti Sakowin Camp, we had good work that was readily accessible, environmentally sustainable, and because it was based in a gift economy, functioned like a living-wage position. The work—whether prepping food, chopping wood, sorting donations, mediating conflicts, facilitating ceremonies, or otherwise—affirmed our dignity and our belonging in community, while directly preventing, escaping, intervening in, and transforming violence. Indeed, as unarmed Water Protectors, we had assembled to resist the colonial violence brought forth by the Dakota Access Pipeline and its backers. This work, in affirming our shared humanity, also created a context in which we were less likely to resort to interpersonal violence ourselves, as most of our deepest needs were met, including the need to give of ourselves with generosity and purpose. Indeed, in spite of the violent presence of authorities outside of Camp, I felt safer within the confines of Camp than any other place, before or since.

At Oceti Sakowin Camp, nestled there at the confluence of the Missouri and Cannonball Rivers, I became a devoted abolitionist even before I knew the term. When funds had been gathered to bail a Water Protector out of jail and the conversation turned to who should do the actual bailing, another Water Protector suggested that I do it because I was local and, in their words, a "badass abolitionist minister." As much as I loved that description, it was sort of like being on that landing with my mother decades before. What did "abolitionist" actually mean?

Today, I'm beginning to catch on. As part of Camp life, I experienced the essence of abolition each and every day, especially in its invitation to me, as well as other descendants of white settler colonialism, to join—or rejoin—the human circle. The Standing Rock movement called all human beings, to become Water Protectors ourselves, taking the restorative path of love and abolition.

Restorative justice—which Clyde Grubbs, a Western Cherokee elder, describes as a contemporary term for age-old Indigenous practices—has become central to abolitionist work. These practices have included truth-telling, genuine accountability, and community participation in justice-making. Also rooted in Jewish and Christian prophetic action, restorative justice takes a healing approach. Those who have enacted harm can repair the damage and thus repair the circle. Even more importantly, those who have been harmed can be seen, heard, and centered, guiding the very process of restoration. In cases of interpersonal harm, this process might look like fixing something broken, working to repay an expense, filling a role left empty by your deeds. In cases of systemic harm, this process might look like Oceti Sakowin Camp.

Rattler, an Oglala Lakota member of Camp security who has since become a loved one, speaks of Camp in this way:

> When you come into Camp, you're family. That's why I told the security guys at the gate to say, "Welcome home" to everyone when they came in. When you're at home, that's your family, that's your love. Camp was our *tiyóšpaye*—that's your community; that's what we were. That's what the love was, the family love. I love you because you're family, and we'll defend each other, we'll help each other out. Explaining our justice system, so to speak, is kind of hard to do. It's more just part of life.

As a descendant of settler colonialism—the most annihilating force for Indigenous peoples ever—I have been offered a way by which I can participate in real and authentic repair. As part of the Water Protector movement, I have been welcomed into the *tiyóšpaye*, the rambling extended family. Each time I have cooked, chanted, held signs, given rides, posted bail, gone to court, tended graves, visited people in prison, and shared in collective prayers, Indigenous Water Protectors have offered me a path by which to rejoin the circle, to repair broken relationships—and myself. As a Universalist committed to love and justice, I can scarcely imagine a more abolitionist way of life.

Abolitionist organizer Erin Miles Cloud has said, "Everybody wants safety for someone, somewhere. Abolitionists want safety for everyone, everywhere."[1] No doubt, the Water Protector movement wants safety—including health, wholeness, and vibrant living water—for absolutely everyone, absolutely everywhere.

Still, some folks insist that abolition is naïve, a pipe dream for idealists.

---

[1] Erin Miles Cloud, remarks at UCLA Law Review Symposium Conference (January 2022).

Yet thousands of people have lived it. In the Water Protector movement, we have breathed it, sung it, shared it, dreaming it into life.

Yes, it can be done. Yes, we can do it. Yes, we human beings—we can do it.

When we look at our own lives, really take a look, we can find moment upon moment when we've done the things that somebody said were impossible—whether we've fought for justice, given grace, begun again, or let ourselves imagine another way. In all our sticky humanity, we are the people our planet needs us to be.

Love One Another, indeed.

16

Love and Risk

Robert C. Spirko

Warning: This essay contains reference to and a brief description of gun violence.

> Love, like truth and beauty, is concrete. Love is not fundamentally a sweet feeling; not, at heart, a matter of sentiment, attachment, or being "drawn toward." Love is active, effective, a matter of making reciprocal and mutually beneficial relation with one's friends and enemies. Love creates righteousness, or justice, here on earth. To make love is to make justice. As advocates and activists for justice know, loving involves struggle, resistance, risk.
>
> —Carter Heyward

> Our values are not eternal guarantees of right decisions or of proper analyses; they are calls to action.
>
> —Sharon Welch

This essay began in 2022 on the stage of the Unitarian Universalist Association's General Assembly in Portland,

Oregon, as the Article II Study Commission was presenting versions of our draft language. I was particularly interested in the response to one line: "We are called upon to risk ourselves for love." At the time, I was still heady from reading Sharon Welch's *A Feminist Ethic of Risk*, and I really liked that line, the cadence of it and how it might push us out of our comfort zones.

Reactions to it were mixed, but one stood out: worry that it could be used by abusers to justify bad actions. That comment and others indicated that my level of risk tolerance was not everyone's, a fact which might have made me overlook important implications. I made the case in our discussion of the feedback to drop the line. It seemed to me that more work would need to be done in our faith before we could really understand and endorse that statement, and more discernment needed to happen on my part.

In any conversation about risk, we all bring our particular histories with us. So, really, this essay has an earlier origin point.

* * *

This essay began in 2008, on the floor of the Tennessee Valley Unitarian Universalist Church in Knoxville, Tennessee. I was lying on top of my wife, son, and mother as a man with a shotgun stood in the aisle of the sanctuary about 30 feet from us. Our lives had been spared by Greg McKendry, our usher, who blocked the first blast with his body. As I slowly worked up the courage—it was only a second, but in that icy crystalline moment it felt so much longer—to look around and see if we were at risk of suffering the same fate, I saw several congregants nearer the shooter tackle him and pull him down.

Afterward, I understood several things in a new way. The first is that danger can come to us all, even in places we assumed were among the safest, such as a sanctuary. I learned in that moment that I am fundamentally not in control of risk. In a system built on hate and violence, on externalizing and projecting fear and pain onto others, none of us is. But some of us are at more risk than others. I experienced a crack in the unconscious assumption of safety I had held for a long time. Despite being disabled and having grown up in precarity, my position as a middle-class white man in the United States had given me the ability to assume that I was safe in most situations. What happened at church that day set me up to listen with an open heart as Black people, Indigenous people, and people of color began telling more openly their stories of being at risk in the world. They are well aware of how much a supposedly neutral system—even a well-intentioned system—puts them at risk in many situations. It asks much more from them in terms of risk tolerance than is asked of others in more privileged positions.

In what follows, I want to try to hold in suspension two truths: first, to agree with June Jordan that "as a Black feminist I cannot be expected to respect what somebody else calls self-love if that concept of self-love requires my self-destruction to any degree,"[1] and second, to realize that I am only alive today to write this essay because of an act of self-sacrifice arising out of love. How do we, without self-sacrifice, ask ourselves to take the risks constitutive of Love?

What drew me to Welch's *A Feminist Ethic of Risk* was the light it might shed on that question. In it, she draws the distinction between an ethic of control and an ethic of risk. An ethic of control equates being "responsible"—being serious about a problem—with power over the outcome. We deal with problems by controlling them. It's a feature of systems of power but also of the liberal activist groups which oppose them. It's baked into the culture of white supremacy. Welch draws on her experience in the peace movement for examples. Because one cannot marshal sufficient power to bring down, for instance, the military industrial complex, or even to prevent the United

---

[1] June Jordan, *Civil Wars: Observations from the Front Lines of America* (Beacon, 1981).

States from going to war when all the machinery of government is set on it, that lack of control sets the activist on the course to despair.

So as a counter to that, Welch turns to the writings of Black women, theologians, authors, and activists, who have a long familiarity with struggle in situations in which they do not have, nor could expect, control. A long history of partial successes showed these communities that it was possible to fail and survive, and that it was important to keep striving. They have evolved what Welch calls an ethic of risk: "the fundamental risk . . . is the decision to care and to act although there are no guarantees of success. Such action requires immense daring and enables deep joy."[2] This hope is not an idle hope—it is more akin to what Cornel West describes as the "tragic hope" of Black communities: a hope that knows fully what the history has been, what the failures have been, but also what the successes have been, and thus what remains possible.

As Welch points out, when assessing risks of action, few people ask themselves what the risks are of not acting. But they are profound. "Doing nothing *does harm*: our neutrality helps the oppressors more than the victims of oppression." By not acting, we support the current system, and that system is killing people, wrecking lives, damaging the web of life every day. Adopting an ethic of risk means siding with hope. The driving force that underpins this tragic hope is Love. And Love requires vulnerability.

Vulnerability is simply accepting risk—accepting the possibility of harm. Brené Brown has noted that in both personal and communal settings, we must open ourselves to the other for relationships and trust to develop. We must offer our stories, share control, and accept that we do not have final say over all

[2] Sharon Welch, *A Feminist Ethic of Risk*, rev. ed. (Fortress, 2000).

outcomes. If I am to affirm the other as a full human being with their own agency, I have to accept limits on my own agency.

This loss of control is ripe for abuse by someone with bad intentions, someone who doesn't accept the same boundaries. Also, any responsible discussion of risk has to account for the fact that some people—marginalized people—are more vulnerable than others, through no choice of their own. There is a difference between chosen vulnerability and enforced vulnerability, and we need to pay careful attention to this in our congregations and in the wider world.

One key takeaway from Brown's work is the importance of creating organizations where "armor is not necessary or rewarded,"[3] organizations that create a space for vulnerability and enable risk taking. If we are to be equitable, if we are to be just, we must do so. Thus, a key question is: are our congregations and faith communities creating such spaces?

In a UU setting, covenants help us manage vulnerability by providing a shared holding of boundaries so that individuals can operate with greater vulnerability within that space. Covenants can help mitigate the human risks of opening ourselves up and can further help mitigate the systemic risks, the enforced vulnerability, that minoritized people face in many settings.

Covenants create a voluntary space for accountability. In covenant, we are each accountable to more than each other; we are also accountable to the covenant itself, which transcends any individual. But it is in mutual relationships with others that we experience that accountability. We are held by and we hold ourselves to our agreements and ideals. A covenant is in part a person taking responsibility for a collective agreement. Covenants are thus engines of accountability; this mutual accountability powers trust. And this trust is what moves us forward. The Beloved Community can never be reached

---

[3] Brené Brown, "Dare to Lead Hub," brenebrown.com.

without this trust, and we cannot reach trust without shared accountability.

Covenant requires commitment. Welch points out, "As long as some people think they can leave, the trust necessary for genuine conversation is impossible. Those who are being helped cannot trust either that they will be heard or that, if they speak honestly, the group that has more privilege will stay in the conversation." Covenants are ways of agreeing not to leave, to stay in community until relationship can be established or re-established.

Participation in a community and with other communities also requires giving up control. In order to genuinely respect the worthiness and dignity of another person or community, we must give up our illusions of control over the relationship. We must work *with* them and not *for* them.

A fear of accountability is a fear of vulnerability, of giving up control to another. As Welch says,

> For some, sharing power seems like death, a loss of self rather than an invitation to explore an alternative construction of selfhood. For some, explorations of alternative structures of persuasion and self-critique seem like the abandonment of reason rather than the entry into a larger conversation.

The more practice we have with covenant, the more practice we have staying in community, even with people we don't have a covenantal relationship with. Our congregations are spaces where we learn the art of risk, of trust, of relationship.

Vulnerability amplifies accountability which amplifies trust which opens space for greater vulnerability, creating a feedback spiral. "The public that emerges from mutually accountable work and dialogue is mutually transformative." This is how we build Beloved Community.

***

The question of self-sacrifice still haunts me. Accepting risk means accepting the possibility of harm to yourself. Welch's way around this is to posit self-love as a counterweight to risk. Respecting yourself, your needs, and your boundaries will help mitigate the danger of self-destruction. And this is very true, most of the time. Side With Love offers *good resources and workshops* on congregational risk discernment; these are important. "The goal is always to live to fight another day," says Rev. Elizabeth Nguyen, in her excellent resources on risk.[4] This is absolutely true.

And yet, I think of Greg McKendry, the usher who saved me. He did not live to fight another day. He did not engage in a careful consideration of his risk tolerance before he acted. Love did not save him. At the same time, the actions that he and others undertook saved many others. Lying on top of my wife, son, and mother, I had no guarantees that I would leave that room. Or even, in sacrificing myself, that I'd save them. A shotgun is a powerful weapon. And yet, there I was. And there Greg was, a few feet away, on the floor.

But also, a few more feet away on the floor, were John Bohstedt, Robert Birdwell, Arthur Bolds, Terry Uselton, and Jamie Parkey; they had dragged the shooter down and piled on top of him to restrain him. They were uninjured, and it was through their quick and decisive action that the lives of many others were saved.

Love cannot promise us safety, but we cannot have safety without it.

I think of Rev. Gordon Gibson, for fifteen years the only Unitarian Universalist minister in Mississippi. Gordon was sent to Selma a month before the march that we've all heard about, sent by the UUA to observe the movement. He spent a week in

[4] Elizabeth Nguyen, "*Risk, Courage and Discernment: Spiritual Preparation,*" Love Resists, uua.org/loveresists.

jail there because of it. He undertook the same risks as James Reeb; he survived. He told me once that it was common, when he was in Mississippi, for ministers of other denominations to come to him and ask him to be the spokesman for one issue or another. "They stood with me—well, a little behind me," he said with his characteristic twinkle, "they had my back, but needed me to take the risk in front." I think also of Gordon's wife, Judy, who gave up a career in biology to be a minister's wife and take on the same risks he did. And I think of them dancing joyfully to Kool and the Gang's "Celebration" at General Assembly 2017.

I think of the First Unitarian Church in Louisville, Kentucky, who put their church building on the line to shelter protestors kettled by the police. There were moments of real risk there—of damage to their building, to their reputation, to their relationship with the police and city government. There was also real risk to the safety of the church members in the building. Church leaders said in interviews that when they offered the church as a sanctuary space, they had no idea the scope of what would be asked of them. And yet they provided it in that moment, and by doing so, they prevented injury, arrest, or possibly death, given the scale of the police brutality that night.

So what do we do? How do we manage in the absence of guarantees? How do we balance the need for self-protection with what Love sometimes demands of us in terms of risk?

Rev. Nguyen's insight can help us: the *goal* cannot be self-sacrifice. The *goal* should be survival to fight another day. We have to be *ready*, however, to encounter the risk boldly should it be necessary. Here's where another key insight from Rev. Nguyen is important:

> Some people with privilege and access to stability . . . perceive risks of participating in direct action to be higher than they are. They are often taught to weigh the risks of action but not the risks of inaction. They are often less experienced in how

> their courage and fear show up. Some people with less privilege and with less access to stability and resilience practices are well practiced in risk assessment and the realities of the violence of inaction. They are often more experienced with how their courage and fear shows up.

This is why Welch had to turn to the writings of Black women: they were better practiced in risk assessment. They were more experienced in courage. We should keep in mind that this shows us a real, practical benefit for us of supporting leadership from historically marginalized and at-risk groups. They often have more realistic assessments of risk based on their individual and community histories.

It's important here not to exoticize or fetishize; as Rev. Nguyen carefully says, "some" are well practiced, not "all." And yet, our caution must not stop us from recognizing the prophetic voices and leadership in our midst.

We must live with no guarantees; we may be called to pay a high price for Love. All we can do is be prepared to love as the times require. By contrast, we do know the high cost of living without Love: shame, guilt, silence, death. Our leaders can help us understand this dual truth.

Ultimately, we need to practice risk. The more we practice, the better our skills and discernment become. We need to prepare for those moments when we have to take action, when the risks of not acting are greater than those of action. We need practice, especially, with institutional risk. Many among us might accept a level of personal risk in our Love work; are we also ready to accept institutional risks? That determination takes careful group discernment, but also collective boldness. We have sometimes sheltered our institutions behind individual risk taking. It is worth thinking about when those relations might be reversed.

I will be honest: being laid so utterly bare to the whims of chance is soul shaking. And I can tell you that after such moments, what is salvific is community. Care. Love. Friends and family reaching out. Other local churches, synagogues, mosques publicly supporting and providing care for us at Tennessee Valley. National UUA leadership and staff coming on site. We were held by so many circles of Love. And this suggests a further insight: after discernment, it is not for everyone, as Rev. Gibson says, to stand in front. It is still risky, and it is still loving, to be there and to hold those who do. Our faith needs fools for Love—wise fools, but fools nonetheless—and it also needs those who can hold them in Love, who can lift them when they fall.

By calling us into wider circles of community, Love empowers us to act; any action puts us at risk. The feedback spiral of Love, risk, and trust—of relationship and community—becomes the ground for the actions that are necessary for mutual liberation. These actions set the conditions for further change and growth, often regardless of their "success" or "failure." And while we know we will never fully arrive at a perfect Beloved Community, we call it into being whenever we accept risk and act in Love, stronger and stronger with each call.

17

When Love Is Criminalized

Rev. Elizabeth Nguyen

By the time my daughter was born, we had lost abortion.

Her birth was an act of love.

The abortion I had before her was also an act of love.

I had my abortion the day that former President Trump announced he was coming for birthright citizenship. The previous day, I had coordinated a direct action against then Attorney General Jeff Sessions. After the two ministers disrupting his speech were dragged out by security and we'd thrown together a press release from a coffee shop nearby, I walked down the street to buy a pregnancy test. I took it that night between strategy calls. The next morning, after accompanying one of the ministers to a CNN interview about the action, I went to my office at the Unitarian Universalist Association and called Planned Parenthood.

Because I was in Massachusetts and it was 2018, it was as easy as any other healthcare appointment. I gratefully had quality care. I showed up, took a pill, and was given another to take later. I met up with a friend for a vigil against antisemitism mourning the recent shooting at the Tree of Life synagogue, ate poutine, and took the subway home.

By 2023, when my daughter was born, abortion had become criminal in a new way, though full reproductive justice has long been elusive. And abortions will remain much more possible for those with privilege, regardless of what the Supreme Court says. And of course, we will always keep having abortions. As we will always keep acting for love, whatever the laws say.

I know in my own body, and I know when I hold the small, strong body of my daughter, how powerful this act of love was. Love is the principled position that all beings deserve thriving, well-being, and respect. As bell hooks says, "Love is an act of will—namely, both an intention and an action." For me, abortion was safe, affordable, accessible, and supported. I was able to freely take an action for love that so many are criminalized for. Criminalization is the laws, policies, and practices that make an act illegal or treat an act as illegal or criminal. Criminalization can result in arrest, jail, surveillance, convictions. Sometimes the act itself remains legal, but functionally it is treated as criminal or is made totally inaccessible.

***

As I write this in December of 2023, Texas has just enacted SB4, enabling any law enforcement to arrest anyone suspected of migrating without authorization. Brittany Watts has been charged with a felony for having a miscarriage in Ohio. I am visiting my in-laws in Florida, where being transgender, undocumented, and teaching the truth are all being criminalized.

Laws have always and continue to criminalize love.

The love that is caring for our health in body and mind.

The love that is migration.

The love that is teaching and learning and stewarding history.

The love that is feeding the hungry.

The love that is making a home outside when you have none.

The love that is bailing someone out of jail.

The love that is protest.

The love that is self-determination.

The list could go on and on.

Our allegiance cannot be to laws but instead must be to love.

* * *

In 2017, a local union organizer was incarcerated by ICE and started organizing support for people inside of the jail where he was caged. He reached out to a few of us on the outside who were clergy and asked us to begin visiting him. He would pass us names during those visits, telling us who had no one to show up to court with them, who was looking for a lawyer, whose family needed help making rent, who had no commissary money on their books, who had an immigration bond and could be free if they could find the money to pay it. Slowly, we built an anti-deportation network and eventually an immigration bond fund. As we did, I became a person who knew the love that is bonding someone out of immigration jail. Our network became people who knew a power that no one should ever know, the power of paying a ransom to the government for a human's freedom. We became people who knew the power of that first hot meal, of showing someone on a map where we were, how far they had come, of lending a phone so someone could call a loved one and say, "I'm out, I'm free." Our bookcases filled with art made by folks while in jail, our guest rooms filled with new friends staying for a few days or weeks or years, our Whatsapps filled with freedom selfies and follow-ups—what needed to be filed now, with what court, what challenge was next. A few years later, I started working for the National Bail Fund Network and its host Community Justice Exchange, supporting other people like myself who had started immigration bond funds around the country.

* * *

In recent years, community members who share resources outside the state through mutual aid, including paying bail or bond, have experienced escalated targeting and criminalization. In 2023, sixty-one protestors were indicted in a document more than a hundred pages along. Among many other claims, the indictment asserted that the defendants had spread ideas such as "collectivism, mutualism/mutual aid and social solidarity." In other words, they were criminalized for the very human desire to support one another. This indictment is part of the repression of the "Stop Cop City" movement, which aims to protect the Weelaunee forest and prevent it from being destroyed to build a police training behemoth. Of those sixty-one, three are volunteers with the Atlanta Solidarity Fund who were also indicted on money laundering and charity fraud charges. These volunteers had committed the "crime" of bailing out those protesting Cop City and others jailed in pretrial detention. We know it is legal to pay bail and bond since bails and bonds are set by the criminal and immigration systems themselves. We know the Atlanta Solidarity Fund did not engage in money laundering and charity fraud and racketeering. And still, these acts of targeted repression by the state have far-reaching consequences. On a recent call, one of our member funds in Texas shared that because of the labyrinth of laws criminalizing immigration and those who could be construed to be aiding immigrants, many are afraid to volunteer with or support their fund.

It's chilling to read this indictment and so many other legal documents that turn acts of humanity into crimes. In the weeks following the indictment, the words that were meant to target, repress, and punish reassembled in my mind into prayer:

Prayer for the not guilty.

Pray for all of us who are not guilty.

Not guilty of collectivism.

Not guilty of social solidarity.

Not guilty of mutual aid.

Pray for all of us who are not guilty of an overt act in furtherance of a forest.

Pray for all of us who are not guilty of an overt act in furtherance of freedom from police brutality.

Pray for all of us who are not guilty of an overt act in furtherance of freedom from prisons.

May we be guilty of the belief "that individuals will work together and voluntarily contribute their own resources to ensure that each individual has its own needs met."

May we be guilty of "the idea of human altruism; that is, individuals will voluntarily offer goods, services, and resources without anything compelling it."

May we dream guilty dreams of "the elimination of police forces in their entirety" and "the protection of the environment."

May we be taught by our people who have had to learn how to survive a cage, a warrant, an indictment, a repression, a backlash to an uprising.

In furtherance of interdependence:

Aid freely and mutually given.

In furtherance of freedom.

In furtherance of forest.

May we fight for the guilty.

May we pray for the not.

***

There are many who aim to transform our world through the reform of laws, who resist the criminalization of abortions and mutual aid through laws and in the courts. Of course we should. I and many others have benefited immensely from legal reforms. Changed laws allowed my father to get a refugee visa, my husband to apply for immigration relief, allowed me to take paid leave after the birth of our child, allowed me to begin and end a domestic partnership, to vote and do a million other acts that are intimate, quotidian, and miraculous. And in so many realms, the changes in laws have made individual lives better. And in so many realms they have not transformed our collective life. For example, there have been thousands of changes to the criminal punishment system over the years, with the supposed goal of making it more fair, more merciful, less violent toward poor people and people of color. And the number of people incarcerated continues to increase. The same could be said for the many attempts to create more economic justice and to narrow the gap between the poor and the rich. Why do we keep trying to change unloving laws when it does not seem to change the outcomes? Particularly in the immigration and pre-trial detention contexts, we have begun to question the courts themselves, alongside the cops and cages we have long sought to abolish. What does a world beyond courts look like? The academic and activist Angélica Cházaro warns us against fighting for "due process deportations," court proceedings that have all the trappings of fairness and process but in the end are destined to end in deportations. When asylum seekers face judges with a 70-percent or higher denial rate or are deported directly from the border without ever seeing a judge, it matters little whether someone has a powerful case, a skilled attorney, or well-prepared evidence. All people are guaranteed representation by an attorney in criminal court, but this has done little to curb the number of people incarcerated and criminalized. Of course, we still want individuals to have every possible tool to fight for their freedom in the current system. But the court itself begins to feel like a performance, one in which we already know the outcome but collectively pretend it's worth going through the motions of the fight each time.

These days, I confess I do not know what a law is. Why are the parents of a trans teen seeking gender-affirming health care or someone driving their undocumented friend or a mom who is miscarrying treated as criminals? Why are those who do violence on behalf of a government not? Why are leaders who have well-documented histories of violence against women and nations and earth itself winning the game of laws as every day so many others lose? In other words, as we often say in my work, laws are just vibes. Laws and the courts where they are operationalized are so often a charade that indicates more about who has power than justice or ethics. It could be scary to consider that these structures we have been taught to rely on are so broken that we should begin again rather than continuing to try to fix them.

And yet, as Unitarian Universalists, we know something about life beyond laws. Our religion is not one of laws. Instead, we center covenants. Promises we make to each other. We are those promise-making, promise-breaking, promise-remaking people. We believe not in rules but in practices and shared behaviors. We live from our own moral compass with love at its center. We understand that all ethics take place in context and that any rule or law can be weaponized against the least powerful. So we focus on embodying love with our actions.

* * *

We are not the first or last to contend with laws against love. Since the beginning of laws, there have been laws that criminalize love: Laws against interracial marriage, laws against queer marriage, laws against holding land in common, laws against speaking languages, dancing dances, practicing spiritual practices. This is nothing new. Gratefully, our resistance isn't either. In my time in Florida, I find not only laws against love, but those who now and through history insist on acts of love. I visit the annual Miccosukee Indian Arts and Crafts Festival in the Everglades. It's a celebration of the art, foodways, way of life, and culture of the descendants of the hundred Miccosukee who refused the Trail of Tears and escaped south, avoiding genocidal removal, carving out a free life in the River of Grass. Between the fashion show of traditional and contemporary clothing designs and the alligator wrestling, the sun setting pink and gold over the vast lushness of the Glades, there is a man wearing a "Teach banned history" button. Amidst criminalization, resistance.

Now many Unitarian Universalists are joining a coalition of progressive faith groups and mutual care networks to provide transportation and homestays to immigrants, trans people, and pregnant people leaving home to seek safety and care.

Unitarian Universalist congregations give haven to medics and protestors in the midst of uprisings and repression. Unitarian Universalists raise money for bail, pay bail, give mutual aid. Unitarian Universalists grapple with the nuance and complexity of which compromises and reforms to support and which to reject as we organize amidst ballot initiatives, candidates and state and federal legislation.

As Unitarian Universalists, we take action when acts of love are uplifted, honored, and supported. And we take action when those acts of love become crimes in the laws of this land. And as so many of us experience, some of us are criminalized regardless of our actions, simply for being. For being alive and Black or alive and queer or alive and a woman or alive and disabled or alive and fat or alive and trans or alive and Muslim or alive and Indigenous or alive and a teenager. Unitarian Universalists are people of love. Our love demands an allegiance to each other, even as systems around us collapse, criminalize, and surveil. We must go toward each other to organize systems of support, connection, and resistance. And we must love, especially when that love is criminalized.

We do all of this imperfectly. We try to understand our different roles, depending on whether we are more or less privileged, more or less criminalized for just being who we are. We use all of our tools—including the laws and the courts. We choose to be strategic, knowing their fallibility, and how overwhelmingly laws are used to criminalize. We are honest about the limits of legal reforms and how they will be attacked and weaponized. We also realize that the system of laws itself may not be redeemable. That we may need to begin anew. And in the long tradition of civil disobedience, we may need to break the laws against love that keep us from surviving and thriving.

And the good news is that we do this every day. People navigate criminalization every day. People love despite unloving laws every day. People recognize that something is not working and begin anew every day. Another one of our theological cores as Unitarian Universalists is that revelation is not sealed; there are always new truths being learned. I can hardly imagine getting rid of laws and courts and beginning from nothing but vision. But then again, here is this baby, learning about the world from nothing but vision. Together each day, we create the reality of her world. We decide how we behave, how we relate to each other, what happens when someone hurts someone else, what is right and what is wrong. We do this every day in our congregations and our communities. We do this when we decide to understand ourselves in our full humanity, not by how we have been criminalized or not. We do this when we decide to humbly take on principled actions that are wrongly criminalized in service of our collective thriving. We do this when we decide that we will make decisions by love and not by law.

***

I took my child Elena, born of my love and the love that is the abortion I had before her, to see the great freedom fighter Harriet Tubman's handkerchief. There it was, in the National Museum of African American History and Culture, close enough to touch. Only a pane of glass between my fingers and her handkerchief, intimate, quotidian, and miraculous. Maybe for when she had a cold or allergies or tears. Everything about Harriet's love was criminalized. Her freedom and what she did to free others.

I showed Elena the handkerchief and I told her:
Some laws against love, we will change.
Some laws against love, we will break.
Let us live by love and not by law.
Let us keep covenant.

Author's note: As of January 2024, SB4 has gone into effect in Texas, the Georgia legislature has effectively outlawed bail funds, and the South Bend Commons, a mutual aid space in Atlanta that provides groceries, masks, yoga, martial arts classes, and a library to the community, was raided by the FBI and Atlanta Police Department.

18

From Longing to Fully Living

Rev. Mykal O. Slack

Love will guide us, peace has tried us,
hope inside us will lead the way
on the road from greed to giving.
Love will guide us through the hard night.

When I sing this hymn by Sally Rogers, I'm often asking myself, *guide us to what? And why?* I recognize the cynicism tied up in these questions. I've heard too many stories and sat pastorally with too many people in the wake of horrific behavior they experienced in our UU congregations not to feel that. We have to concern ourselves with how much we are or are not connecting the dots between the words we use and the responsibility our faithful witness calls us into as a result of having used those words. Addressing that concern is worth every bit of our time, if Unitarian Universalism is meant to live out the very best parts of itself within our own hearts, in the confines of our churches, and out in the public square.

The truth is that attempting to write about love in this moment has touched a profound sadness in me that I wasn't expecting. Not so much because I believe love is missing in the contours of our faith, but because I don't believe we have figured out how to live what we've named as most precious. Love is central to a faith and worldview that is supposed to make way for all of us to be our whole selves, and to bring our whole selves to the project of getting free together. But as a Black person who ministers with intention to Black people in our faith, I can tell you that Black people cannot be and bring our whole selves here. Neither can those of us who are trans and nonbinary. Neither can people with disabilities. Or poor, underemployed, or unhoused people. And god forbid someone show up with any combination of these identities and lived experiences. So what does all this talk of love really mean?

Perhaps the naming of love as our central value is a deep expression of longing more than it is anything exacting or clear. It makes sense. We have all longed for love and care, a sense of belonging, and a place that we can truly call home in virtually every aspect of life. We need these things as much as we need food, clean air and water, and shelter. Poet and activist adrienne maree brown suggests, in a piece called "longing," that an all-encompassing love is "the only privilege I have seen have universal positive impact in the world." [1]

Many of us found Unitarian Universalism precisely because there were no clear pathways to fulfilling these needs in other faith traditions. Many of us remain in Unitarian Universalism, despite those needs not being met in the ways we longed for because we believe in the power and possibility of love to help us shift course. Perhaps our longing, despite what Unitarian Universalism means to each of us individually, is a place of collective alignment that can orient us toward the justice-making, equity, transformation, pluralism, interdependence, and generosity articulated by the revisions of Article II.

But we can't stop there. Understand me. There's nothing wrong with a deep desire to put love at the center of all we do, say, and believe as Unitarian Universalists. Longing is often a vehicle for imagination, (re)direction, and change, and it can be the energy that drives us toward becoming more of who we say we want to be, both within our congregations and affiliated organizations and out in the world. But the low buzz of a hoped-

[1] adrienne maree brown, "Longing," adriennemareebrown.net (December 9, 2012).

for future without a deeper call and commitment to act in the here and now can lead to the stagnancy and irrelevance of a dying church. What's the bridge? How do we move from longing for to fully living into what is truest and best about our faith? How do we shift from what's aspirational and pretty (from a distance) to what's tangibly real and understandably messy (up close)? How do we push ourselves and one another out of the staleness of striving to an ethic and ethos of arriving?

If longing is the spiritual and emotional tug of love, then risk-taking is the tangible, accountable embodiment of that love. It means saying the hardest things, the things that get to the heart of our UU values, in the hardest moments, even when it might also mean losing people we care about or ceding our own power and authority. It means not running from conflict because staying in the work of long-term re-alignment and reconnection is more important than smoothing things over for short-term comfort.

A faithful embodiment of love at the center isn't a *check a box and move on* kind of endeavor. It is a *prepare a place for those who've not yet arrived* kind of effort. This is the work of a lifetime, with endless reminders that the work won't ever be finished in a world like the one we're living in. Yet love calls us to be steadfast because of what's possible in the long run by our diligence and our care. Love focuses us on what our values require of us instead of the words we choose to express them. Faithful embodiment of our values is about impact on relationships and community-building and on bridging the gaps between who we are and who we are called to be.

In many ways, Article II's revisions speak to the challenge and hope in Sharon Welch's *A Feminist Ethic of Risk*, in which she calls for a redefinition of and reorientation to responsible action by moving from an ethic of control to an ethic of risk. Welch describes the ethic of control as steeped in quick and predictable responses, conceptualizations of freedom that are individualistic and not communal, scarcity thinking, and transactional relationships in the context of systems that do not take into account the fullness of who we are as people. By stark contrast, her ethic of risk involves a deep and honest engagement with the complexities of our varied lived experiences, creativity and innovation in the work, belief in abundance and possibility, and vigor and commitment proportional to the stakes. We must act as if our very lives, as well as the lives of our loved ones, co-workers, and community members, depend on it because they actually do.

Welch writes,

> This literary, ethical, spiritual, and philosophical tradition is compelling for two reasons: first, it offers a profound critique of the systemic and cultural distortions and costs of racism [and other forms of oppression] that [all people] need to hear and understand. Second, it provides narratives of engaged goodness: there are no heroic pretensions, no grand narratives of certain triumph, but a life-affirming refusal to submit to cynicism, alienation, and despair.[2]

As I think about what's possible when we lean into risk, I am reminded of my summer internship in 2006 at a UCC church in Western Massachusetts. Part of my time there was spent developing a workshop series on transgender experience and spirituality. I was newly transitioning in my gender expression, and the hope of that project was to help the people of the church both understand my own lived experience and provide meaningful support and spiritual care to a growing population of trans people moving to the surrounding areas. By midway through the summer, I was able to offer the series over a period of four Sundays after worship.

That first Sunday, about thirty-five people gathered for the workshop. The first to arrive were a couple in their eighties, longtime members of the congregation who I'd spoken to often

[2] Sharon Welch, *A Feminist Ethic of Risk*, rev. ed. (Fortress, 2000).

on Sundays. The discussion was lively and hope-filled; we moved through the first session with a lot of questions and grace, and I reminded folks that we had three more opportunities to connect, learn, and grow together.

After everyone else had gone, the couple approached me and asked to chat. It turned out that they had a trans daughter who lived in a neighboring town. They hadn't spoken to her in fifteen years. They told me about how stuck they'd been and how there didn't seem to be any way for them to reconnect with her. And although they weren't sure how, they had renewed faith that something could be different; they were willing to do whatever it took to rebuild the relationship.

I asked the couple if they had contacted their daughter during their estrangement; they had not. I suggested that they call and offered to coach them about how to approach the moment. As uncomfortable as I knew they were, they did everything we talked about, risked the potential for more pain on all sides, and ended up leaving a message on their daughter's voicemail one afternoon. They told me that they'd mentioned to her in the message that they were attending the workshop series, had learned some new things, and wanted to talk to her, if she was willing. They acknowledged that the father had said some pretty awful things to her before she left home and so weren't necessarily expecting to hear back from her.

On that third Sunday, the couple arrived early, like usual, and we began our time together, along with the other participants. What we didn't know was that their daughter had listened to the message and had been moved enough by it that she made the decision to attend the workshop that day. I had only seen an old photo of her before transition that the father had kept in his wallet, so I didn't recognize her. They also didn't know she was coming, so imagine their shock and joy when she came in and sat next to them!

That family's time together in that workshop changed all of us. The couple had married in that church, and their daughter was well known in the community. She had been a member in her teens and early twenties, but left the church after she got clear about her gender and didn't find the support and care she needed there. The session ultimately turned into a kind of family reunion. There were so many tears and deep gratitude that they had this opportunity to get to know who she had become. I watched all of them use some of what they had been learning to hold that whole family as they reunited. This singular moment allowed all of the people present to bear witness to possibility when we open ourselves up to it and move from a place of love with intention.

Later that month, I was invited to join a meeting with the parents, their forty-something-year-old trans daughter, and the senior minister, who also remembered the daughter as part of that family. After catching everyone in that meeting up on how she was doing in life, the daughter was able to share how hard it had been for a number of trans folks in the area and asked if the church could provide space for her and some friends to meet monthly. The minister was happy to offer the space for free for as long as they wanted to meet, and a trans support group was born that the daughter led for the ten years that they met in that church.

In *Black Liturgies*, Cole Arthur Riley recognizes that sometimes we need help moving toward a kind of love that is decisive. In this reframing of our core values that Article II's revisions offer us, we have a real opportunity to do and be different; to embody our faith as Unitarian Universalists in ways we, perhaps, have never been able to pull off; and to live into the risk necessary to do so. My hope and prayer is that our collective willingness will outshine our fear and uncertainty.

Will you sing something different with me now?

I am open and I am willing
To be hopeless would seem so strange
It dishonors those who go before us
So lift me up to the light of change . . .

19

Love and Power at the Center

Rev. Mary Katherine Morn

One by one, the sheets were laid over my head as I sat still in a chair. I had seen the powerful demonstration during my own training. And still, I had to work to regulate my breathing. I'm not sure we would ask someone to take that chair in a training today. More is understood about the impact of trauma. And more is understood concerning the dynamics of power and systemic oppression that were the subject of the training. As a relatively new minister, the training planted important seeds for my own growing understanding.

Our experience was the first of its kind—denominationally funded training for a group of ministers on professional boundaries and preventing ministerial misconduct. We would in turn provide opportunities for this learning among our colleagues.

When my partner and I facilitated these spaces, I took the chair for the layers of abuse exercise. A colleague read the brief statements describing a series of sexualized experiences, sexual harassment, and sexual violence, and with each experience another sheet was placed over my head. I didn't expect the weight of the layers. The way each one obscured my senses, each one leaving me feeling a little less able to move on my own. Each one seemingly paralyzing me, creating a sense of personal power taken.

My co-facilitator knew to move quickly to the healing story. As each experience of care, of acknowledgment, of justice was spoken, a sheet was lifted. It was simplistic, in a way. And it also bore a simple and important truth about our humanity; the uncovering revealing again what was there all along—my full humanity and power.

Of course the dynamics of the abuse of power by a spiritual leader is a subject deserving of its own exploration, but this piece of the larger story came to mind in the context of my reflections on the centrality of love, its relationship to power, and love as *action* in the face of injustice; all of this together is one way to describe the call to love embodied in the mission of the Unitarian Universalist Service Committee (UUSC).

Polite Theology Falls Short

Coming up in the embrace of a white Christian theology that centered love—that part about love had always seemed simple to me. The particular theology and the social constructs in which I lived as a child and young adult worked together to make it so, serving to protect my ignorance and "innocence." When I discovered the many privileges I enjoyed that made possible my facile, polite theology of love, I came to see the harm caused by such a theology. This understanding also freed me to imagine the possibility of love as a force that does not depend on me maintaining privilege or a position of superiority that could be lost at any moment. How liberating to know that I do not have to be in constant battle to protect my personal worth and dignity.

Love at the center requires that we fearlessly and joyfully embrace the full humanity of each other and of all.

Through decades of leadership and learning (and still today), teachers and companions have repeatedly invited me to look more deeply in order to see the dehumanizing impacts on all of us created by the systems of supremacy (patriarchy, racism, extractive capitalism, colonialism) that too often order our shared life. Systems of superiority not only create violence and oppression and the denial of the human rights of so many, but also require constant vigilance and a perversion of the humanity of those holding the “privileges” of superiority.

The notion of universal human rights is a rejection of supremacy systems. The protection of universal human rights requires centering of love, with every point on the circle in like relation to the center.

Inherent Dignity and Power

The version of UUSC’s mission statement in use when I became UUSC’s president and lead executive officer in 2018 included an affirmation of the inherent dignity and *power* of all people. It was months after I arrived that I noticed I was not reading the language of Unitarian Universalism’s first Principle, *the inherent worth and dignity of all people.* I can only imagine how many times I shared UUSC’s affirmation incompletely, without *power.* Leaving *power* out is no trivial omission—particularly in the sphere of human rights.

In my six years as witness to the remarkable work of UUSC grassroots partners, it is their power that has moved me the most. With respect and care, I am sharing just a few stories of love and power from our partners.

UUSC’s Theory of Change

After almost three decades of congregational ministry, my on-the-job training for my ministry at UUSC came in earnest at a retreat center an hour outside of Anchorage, Alaska. One of the ways UUSC leverages its position as a small, faith-based human rights organization is by supporting connections among grass-roots organizations. For nearly a year prior to the 2018 convening in Alaska, staff had been facilitating planning meetings with partners from Alaska, Louisiana, the Pacific, and Bangladesh.

As one of the earliest funders of groups addressing climate-forced displacement, UUSC was pleased to respond to partners' requests for this opportunity to learn and strategize together. The leaders of seven organizations planned five days together to build relationships by sharing their stories of climate displacement and creating strategies that would leverage the emerging relationships.

The 2018 convening resulted in a mutually created and adopted Climate Displacement Framework and the vision of a legal justice strategy that has since prompted responses from both the United Nations (UN) and the Inter-American Commission on Human Rights (IACHR). From a five-year vantage point at this writing, the impact of these two work products has been significant. For Indigenous Peoples in the United States, the UN and the IACHR have acknowledged and recognized the grave human rights abuses that Tribal Nations in Alaska and Louisiana are experiencing due to the impacts of climate-forced displacement and have subsequently called on the United States government to address these issues.

Beyond the intended outcomes of the convening, my experience of joining UUSC colleagues in observing and supporting these leaders in Alaska was important in shaping my own leadership at UUSC and my engagement with faith-inspired, values-driven work for global justice. From start to finish of each day, our partners attended to practices that brought us back to the center, to love. And simply put, all of this attention held the unspoken (yet vividly clear) intention of honoring each person's full humanity, dignity, and power, and thereby unfailingly centering love.

Participants and planners set the tone with great care on our first night together. Representatives from the various regions and communities came forward to introduce themselves, to thank our hosts, the Athabascan Indians, and to acknowledge the elders. Offerings were shared—flowers, incense, song. The youngest children present joined their older siblings (tribal, family, spirit); on one occasion a little one took center stage during a dance performed by youth who were undisturbed by the "interruption." The evening's practice of honoring each other and our connection with creation was as powerful as any ritual gathering I have been part of.

What a gift to be introduced to UUSC's commitment to radical trust in relationship with our partners in this way. What a gift to bear witness to and be blessed by the power of the practice of reverence and honor so deeply grounded in Indigenous identity.

The Power and Dignity in Stories of Love and Liberation

One of UUSC's guiding principles[1] is to honor the power and dignity of people's stories. This might seem an odd value to highlight; however, in the context of colonial, white-supremacist, patriarchal, capitalist extractivism, the theft of people's stories is a violation that creates immediate harm and perpetuates oppressive systems.

I was in the retreat center meeting room, listening as Indigenous leaders described the devastating harm of climate change on their communities, watching the slide shows of encroaching water, melting permafrost, storm-wrecked towns, all against the backdrop of the breathtakingly beautiful Alaska landscape, when I came to a deeper understanding about dignity and power. By meeting people with our perception of what they lack, we reinforce supremacy ideologies and systems and do not create conditions for human rights to thrive.

[1] Power and dignity in stories of love and liberation are the threads that weave our vision of human rights for all. We will affirm and amplify the dignity, power, and right to self-determination of our partners, staff, and members when sharing their stories or communicating about our work.

What a privilege it is at UUSC to shift money and other resources to people whose stories of love and liberation are the threads that weave a tapestry of human rights for all. How important it is to be reminded that the work for human rights always starts in the places where rights are most at risk, where people imagine and build toward their own liberation.

Power in Action

In a powerful photo that was shared widely during the 2019 Climate Strike, members of one of the partners with us at the Alaska convening, Pacific Island Climate Warriors, stood knee deep in the Pacific holding a banner that proclaimed their unmistakable spirit: "We are not drowning. We are fighting." I read this as an unimpeachable assertion of self-determination, dignity, and power, and a vehement rejection of the tendency of so many to reduce people who are suffering under systems of oppression to their suffering.

The difficult dynamics of a relatively wealthy western organization providing resources to small grassroots groups advancing human rights are undeniable. We on staff and on UUSC's board strive to be awake and accountable to this, and we are also aware that our privilege will sometimes obscure (to us) the ways we fail. We are grateful for what we learn from partners, and especially for the ways they help us grow in our accountability.

I have found that UUSC partners are not confused about power. In the face of threats to life, livelihood, and safety, activists do not have the luxury of powerlessness or resignation. And further, the fight for rights is always predicated on the affirmation of human dignity. The rejection of a supremacist view requires the acknowledgment of individual power and the right to self-determination.

Changing the World

Twenty-seven young adult law school students have demonstrated for many around the world the potential of people with a vision of justice and equity who know their power. In their environmental law classroom at the University of the South Pacific, the students were given the assignment to imagine the most progressive and ambitious climate change action they could take in the international legal arena. They researched previous actions and campaigns and decided that the United Nation's General Assembly should direct the International Court of Justice to create an advisory opinion on the human rights impacts of climate change and the obligations of states to protect people from past, present, and future harm (how they describe intergenerational equity).

They took their proposal to the Pacific Island Forum and essentially got a nod and a congratulations. But this was not an idle exercise for them; they wanted nothing less than a vote by the UN General Assembly. So they formed the Pacific Islands Students Fighting Climate Change and launched their International Court of Justice Advisory Opinion (ICJAO) campaign.

UUSC was one of the first funders of Pacific Island Students. Solomon and Vishal, campaign directors, told UUSC's Board during a visit in Boston that it was funding from UUSC that made it possible for them to attend COP26 in Scotland and make connections with larger organizations with access to greater funding. UUSC also supported them by providing UN credentials and connecting the leaders with housing in New York during the most intense period of the campaign. (I love the way being a small organization makes small, important things possible.)

With the sponsorship of the nation of Vanuatu, the 27 students took their campaign to the world and ultimately received the support of more than 120 nations, almost two-thirds of the member nations.

On March 29, 2023, the United Nations General Assembly adopted by unanimous consent the Pacific Island Students' proposal. I still involuntarily shake my head a little remembering their remarkable achievement.

One of the things that struck me in my conversations with and observations of the leaders of the PISFCC campaign was the way they brought together an unrelenting seriousness of purpose and unapologetic use of power, with a passionate joy and love for Life.

Their determination reminds me of the words of the Rev. Dr. Martin Luther King, Jr.:

> Power without love is reckless and abusive, and love without power is sentimental and anemic. Power at its best is love implementing the demands of justice, and justice at its best is love correcting everything that stands against love.[2]

Love in Action

Standing in sharp relief against love in our broken and battered world is a stubborn supremacy. Clinging to innocence and deniability, or some sentimental, convenient notion of love that asks little of those who hold privilege, protects the status quo by reducing people impacted by oppressive systems to something quite short of their full humanity.

Layers of violence and diminishment can obscure and paralyze. The collective work of dismantling oppressive systems

---

[2] Martin Luther King, Jr., "Where Do We Go from Here?" speech delivered at the 11th Convention of the Southern Christian Leadership Conference, Atlanta (August 16, 1967).

does not create power, it uncovers it, revealing what was there all along.

Having been founded in the context of Unitarian Universalist histories and theologies means that UUSC inherits and wrestles with the gifts and challenges familiar to many of us. Blessed by a clarity of mission and a commitment to ongoing growth, I hope that UUSC is a beacon for an imperfect practice of centering love. For my own ministry and practice of my faith, it has been a gift to learn and grow in partnership, and a source of hope and courage for love in action.

Imagine love as a force that frees us, each and all, to the fullness of our humanity. Imagine that love centered, at like distance from every point on the circle. Imagine the community care that holds the tension of the circumference *and* the radius.

We know too well the limitations that disrupt right relationship around the circle of humanity. It is the pull toward the center that will hold us together. In the smallest of families or communities, to the most distant and vast global relationships, accountability to every person's full humanity unfailingly centers love.

A final note of thanks to all those, staff, board, and supporters who contribute to our work with partners, advancing human rights. It is a tremendous honor to join you, as together we center love in action.

20

Love, a Work in Process

Rev. Bill Sinkford

The year was 1959. The American Unitarian Association and the Universalist Church of America were meeting together in Syracuse, New York. They were there to vote on joining two iconic American faith communities.

The idea of merger had been on the table since 1865, almost one hundred years. There had been decades of study commissions and thousands of surveys to test grassroots support for and resistance to coming together.

For the merger to become real, both communities had to approve a set of proposed bylaws for the new Unitarian Universalist Association.

Fifty-seven amendments were put forward, voted upon, and passed. Only one outstanding challenge remained. It came down to one word in Article II, in language that would commit the new merged faith to cherish and spread the universal truths taught by the great prophets and teachers of humanity in every age and tradition, immemorially summarized in our Judeo-Christian heritage as love to God and love to man.

Our Judeo-Christian heritage? (Jesus had been mentioned in an earlier version, but the growing humanist sentiment among the Unitarians had ruled that out.) The question was how tightly tethered the new merged faith would declare itself to be to Christianity.

That one word, *our*, focused an essential question of identity. In the middle of the night, an agreement was finally reached to change *our* to *the:* the Judeo-Christian heritage. Sleepless in

Syracuse was the way one article described the drama of that night.

That change of one small word, memorialized in Article II of the new UUA bylaws made the approval of merger possible.

Some of you may have reacted less to the Christian language and more to the male-gendered language in that story, "love to God and love to *man*." In fact, a grassroots movement of UU women and their allies objecting to gendered language fueled the first major revision of Article II, twenty-five years after the Syracuse convention, in 1985.

The question of relationship to the Christian tradition was still live, but the 1985 revision dealt with that by separating the "Sources" on which we rely, from the seven new, non-gendered "Principles."

The new Article II was almost unanimously approved.

But over time, the statement of identity expressed in those seven Principles satisfied more and more Unitarian Universalists less and less. They articulated an ethical identity, not a religious identity. They included not one word of traditional religious language. I raised questions about that when I was president of the UUA, sparking what came to be called the Language of Reverence controversy.

Even the chair of the committee that drafted the Principles doubted many folks would ask for them to be read, for comfort, on their deathbeds.

The Principles were not only abstract, but passive statements, with no verbs, no action words at all, in a faith that prided itself on activism.

But it was not until another grassroots movement, with leadership from members of All Souls in Washington, DC, called us to name the central challenge of racism and reflect on our accountability that energy gathered for a new approach to describe our religious identity.

It was not until hundreds of congregations considered and adopted the eighth Principle, that our larger family of faith decided that we again needed new language to define who we are as religious people.

I offer this short history lesson to make the point that these formal statements of religious identity in our bylaws tend to follow movement within our faith rather than lead it. They have tended to reflect consensus rather than aspiration.

Even the important but less encompassing change reflected in the addition of Earth-centered spirituality to our Sources in 1995 followed the rapidly expanding number of Unitarian Universalists who found meaning in those traditions.

How does change take place in Unitarian Universalism, in this faith community in which the question of religious authority is always on the agenda? We value individualism so very highly. It is no accident that "the inherent worth and dignity" of each individual is our first Principle, interdependence our last. Change almost never comes "top down" in Unitarian Universalism.

Almost all UU congregations light a chalice in worship. No one, no group, told congregations to do that. No General Assembly voted to require a chalice lighting in UU worship.

Spirit of Life is sung in so many congregations. There was no vote at a General Assembly adopting that hymn as our common doxology.

Consensus developed that lighting a chalice could be an important shared ritual. Consensus gathered that Spirit of Life could be a defining element in our worship lives.

You may not consider this discussion of change to be theological, but how we do church and how we change church are central theological questions. I would argue that our practice of this faith is every bit as important as our beliefs and our language.

Several open and active questions (they are called "arguments" in the world of theological discourse) are addressed in the current recommended change: racism and accountability, the limits of individualism and reaction to hierarchy, and yearning for more specifically religious language among them. One question this new approach raises is therefore what consensus has developed or is developing on these religious questions. Have we, for example, moved beyond racial representation as the goal and toward dismantling the broader culture of white supremacy? Are we ready to consider the place of ordination in a religious culture where shared and lay leadership is the increasing priority?

Our history does not ask what stone tablets we should chisel, what transcendent and unchanging truths we should embrace, but what questions we should be asking. These questions locate our reflection in a theological world of process.

You've probably heard the self-deprecating commentary common among us: "Process is our most important product." Perhaps that, however, is not a weakness, just a difference from other ways to be religious. Perhaps it is in fact one of our great strengths, if we would embrace it. "Revelation is not sealed" is a fundamental part of the way we live as religious people, despite our yearning for certainty and our attachment to the familiar.

With all of these questions alive among us, a new approach to describing our religious identity was needed, just as the Principles were a new approach back in the 1980s.

A proposal was developed by a committee, presented at the Pittsburgh General Assembly, and approved for a year of study. The 2024 GA adopted the new language by more than the required two-thirds margin. Our foundational language is driven democratically, from the grassroots up.

But these statements reflect movement of the spirit that is already taking place among us, in our covenanted communities and in our complicated spiritual lives. They are a reflection of where the spirit has led us so far. They are not dictated by any authority other than our own lives. They are useful and have authority only to the extent that they reflect who we understand ourselves to be. The new proposal has many things to recommend it, in my view:

- It is clearly a statement of religious, not just ethical, identity.
- It speaks to values, not abstract principles.
- The values listed are interdependent, not listed with individualism at the top.
- The new language includes plenty of verbs, calling for reflection and for action. Our anti-oppression and anti-racism commitments are infused throughout. In the language of this proposal:

  > Systems of power, privilege, and oppression have traditionally created barriers for persons and groups with particular identities, ages, abilities, and histories. We pledge to replace such barriers with ever-widening circles of solidarity and mutual respect.

- Rather than a list of sources, the proposal offers a statement of *inspiration*:

  > As Unitarian Universalists, we use, and are inspired by, sacred and secular understandings that help us to live into our values. We respect the histories, contexts and cultures in which they were created and are currently practiced.
  >
  > [We are] Grateful for the religious ancestries we inherit and the diversity which enriches our faith . . . .

- Most importantly, love is at the center:

  > Love is the power that holds us together and is at the center of our shared values. We are accountable to one another for doing the work of living our shared values through the spiritual discipline of Love.

  What might it mean to put love at the center? Has that become a consensus among us?

The first thing to note is that, in many ways, love is already at the center of our Unitarian Universalist community, culture, and language. How many of you have one of those yellow shirts with "Side with Love" in big letters across the front? When we arrive at protests, people often say, "Here come the Love people."

Centering love associates Unitarian Universalism with its greatest recent achievements (gay and lesbian empowerment) and most effective witness for justice (in the struggle for marriage equality).

And *Beloved Community* is important language for us. It is in the mission statement of many UU congregations. *Beloved Community* associates this faith with Dr. King, with the Civil Rights victories of the last century.

It is not hard to argue that putting love at the center recognizes movement and change that is already in process. It is possible to view love at the center as reflecting a consensus that has already substantially developed among us.

I want to test that proposition, however, in several ways.

First, past victories can be important in shaping identity. But the marriage equality movement did not address transphobia or provide much wisdom in the shifting expression of gender and gender identity. It did not offer a collective critique of the gender binary or even critique of the institution of marriage.

The ending of legal apartheid, as important as that was, left this country with the culture of white supremacy still in place, still in need of a Black Lives Matter movement.

Can placing love at the center both affirm progress we have been a part of but also call us to engage the challenges ahead? Can Article II be more than a statement of consensus already reached? Can Article II ask us for faithfulness as we move into uncharted theological and political territory?

This is where the values that surround love in this new approach can help. Inseparable from one another, these shared values are justice, generosity, pluralism, transformation, equity, and interdependence.

Perhaps, if we can hold an aspiration this complex, it will work against the kind of weaponizing of the Principles I've seen in so many church conflicts. You've seen it too—how my "inherent worth and dignity" has been hurled against your commitment to "democratic process" or your belief in "justice, equity and compassion." Perhaps statements of religious identity this complex will lead us into deeper reflection rather than more unproductive argument. Can this one function as aspiration, calling us into deeper reflection, as well as confirmation of our past success?

Can this statement of religious identity go beyond the lowest common denominator among us, calling this faith to wrestle with questions about which consensus has not developed?

Most of us, with the experience of relational intimacy as our most powerful reference, know that love is not just a warm feeling. Our most powerful experience of love leaves no doubt that love requires real effort, that to love is a decision not a condition.

But is the language of love just a cipher, a way to suggest a higher power, to suggest God, while avoiding that word which remains loaded for many among us?

The Gospel of John offers the succinct opinion that "God is love." One theologian I have learned from suggests that love is "the least worst way to talk about God." Or we could call it the least worst way to talk about the mystery that transcends our individual lives. Even that language is, I know, a challenge for some among us.

What is this love that we would place at the center of our concern? And how does it work? Does this love have power? Does it desire a particular outcome?

Or is this love partnering with us, or perhaps even entirely dependent on us?

Would placing love at the center allow us to claim a collective vision and a knowing that there is a better way to live?

Could it be that placing love at the center would simply allow us to gather confidence in possibilities that we can only glimpse? Might its value be in sharpening our focus on what we hold to be of ultimate importance?

Could putting love at the center be a fundamental act of faith? Could it be an act of resistance that rejects the way things are as the best that they can be?

Could Article II become less a consensus statement about the way things work and more a commitment to help things work differently?

Could this new approach point us toward hope?

We have been exploring how the Principles can help us live faithful lives in a difficult world for almost 40 years. It is important to remember that foundational language takes time to live into. It is also important to remember that it is likely to be around for a long time.

For years, many of us were able to convince ourselves that progress toward the Beloved Community was almost inevitable if we worked for it—until recent years . . . .

But today, we know that we are going to need a faith that can sustain us in the face of reversals. The last question for all of us is not whether we place the word *love* at the center of some graphic that will live on some website.

The real question is whether we can experience and find joy in a love that holds us and can help us live as we want to live, even in a world that is demonstrably indifferent to suffering.

May the answer to that question be yes.

Ashe and Amen.

21

On Love

Rev. Marco Belletini

> The practice of love offers no place of safety.
> We risk loss, hurt, pain. We risk being acted
> upon by forces outside our control.
>
> —BELL HOOKS

The religious congregation I attended as a child was a large parish church, Roman Catholic, in Detroit, Michigan. The parish had about 25 thousand persons back in the 1950s and seven services on Sunday. The sermon, aka homily, was about ten minutes long and the service exactly an hour, with fifteen minutes between the later morning services to navigate the nightmare of parking ins-and-outs.

I didn't go there looking for principles to live my life by or a creed to make sense of it, but simply because my parents took me.

As a child, I recited or chanted the credo (in the staccato Latin back then), which was just a string of rhythmic phonemes to me. Of course, I was taught about the meaning of creed over time in the parochial school I attended. But even then, not all of it made any sense to me. "Et expecto resurrectionem mortuorum" was not difficult Latin to figure out because of all the cognates, but the idea of "expecting" the dead to climb out from their graves seemed like Greek mythology to me.

My parents had no religious education when they grew up. They just went to Mass and heard the same words over and over without really knowing much of what they meant. Even when the creedal words "genitum non factum" changed to English in the 1960s, the translation "begotten, not made" was hardly a phrase that defined them as Catholic or drew them into more participatory church community. For that matter, with 25 thousand folks in the church, six priests, ten nuns, and a number of different services, they never even saw the same people from week to week. Church was not about community for them, but simply part of the identity of being Italian. You prayed the rosary at home, said your Ave Marias, and put two dollars in the basket on Sunday.

When I started going to a Universalist Unitarian church in my early twenties, I retained my Italian identity but had already given up everything that I had come to understand in the Catholic creed through my education. The congregation I attended was *much* smaller, very old, and had proudly played a role in the Underground Railroad. They drank coffee together after the service.

The service in that church had no creed, affirmation, or set of principles on the wall. I didn't go because of belief or unbelief anyway, but because a good friend married to a close friend from high school had been raised Unitarian Universalist; and I found her to be a wonderful, sane person. I sought out a community where my rather inarticulate agnostic inner life might be in community with others. We never said a covenant like "Love is the doctrine of this church," but we did sing beautiful hymns, often with beautiful lines that stirred me, awed me, and even sometimes confirmed that my own inner life actually did overlap the inner life of others in the congregation.

The minister explained that *Unitarian* originally referred to the belief that God is a Unity rather than a Trinity, and that Universalism was a belief in universal salvation, no hell in other words, but then he pointed out that no one that he knew in the congregation even "believed" in God or thought that there was anything beyond death, not just no hell but no heaven either.

Eventually I entered the path to serve a Unitarian Universalist congregation as a minister myself, three years, a heart-shattering experience, and lots of self-reflection later.

I don't remember ever once hearing an affirmation, creed, or so-called covenant like "Love is the doctrine of this church" in the congregations I served as a student minister or an intern, each in a different part of the country. I never used any such thing in any of the chapel services at Starr King School for the Ministry, and yet there were strong communities in both congregations and the school. People attended such services, it seemed to me, more for the community and the shared art-form of worship than any common recited set of beliefs or unbeliefs, although they sometimes used vocabulary at the very edge of "traditional" Christian and Jewish sensibilities, like *grace*, or *love*, or *deep* or *holy* now and then, or even *spiritual*, but hardly in the sense that word is used today as in the phrase "spiritual, but not religious."

When I visited other congregations where everyone there rose and recited from memory, "Love is the doctrine of this church, the quest for truth its sacrament . . . . ," it reminded me of rising and saying words from memory as a young Catholic boy. But the words didn't particularly create community for me or deepen and help me make meaning of my actual lived life.

Over time, I became more involved in the words used in our common worship when I served on the Hymnbook Resources Commission back in the 1980s.

We received literally thousands of suggested hymns and songs, and we sang every single one. We were surprised by the number of texts sent to us, both for song texts and worship usage, that contained nothing more than a few abstractions: *Let us Love everyone. Let us all be free. We are a people of truth and justice!*

No imagery. Few concrete nouns. Just the abstract words. Nothing but the assumption that we all know what *love, freedom,* and *justice* means and have experienced all these concepts in similar and defining ways. These seemed to us to be "feel good" abstractions with shine but no depth, push, pull, gravity, or fire.

I suppose some of these submissions were in response to the heated conversations and serious conflicts of the mid 1980s. New feminist insight about how the English was used in our preaching and worship stirred up a lot of heated engagement. The hymns and songs we sang from *Hymns for the Celebration of Life* used the word *man* often to refer to humankind, and male pronouns dominated. Most of the sources of hymns and words were male, as well. And there were no words at all, nor music at all, from Black sources of any gender. Not one.

And one of my co-workers at Hawthorn Center for Emotionally Impaired Children, where I once worked, often quoted Dr. Martin Luther King, teaching me how white English often degrades racial language:

> Somebody told a lie one day. They couched it in language. They made everything black ugly and evil. Look in your dictionary and see the synonyms for the word black. It's always something degrading, low, and sinister. Look at the word white. It's always something pure, high, and clean. Well I wanna get the language right, tonight. [1]

Although many of our ministers marched with King at Selma, at home, our congregations were centers where the language was both male and utterly white. The conversations about race in our congregations were just getting started. And

---

[1] Martin Luther King, "I'm Black and I'm Beautiful" (speech delivered August 11, 1967), youtube.com.

already the conversations among women in our movement were mostly different than conversations among men at the time.

But which theological words we were to use in worship demanded a lot *more* conversation and attention in those days. The use of the word *God* in a sermon, or the mention of Jesus (except at Christmas perhaps), made choppy waves among members in the largest number of our congregations. Another set of congregations used a variety of transcendental metaphors, such as "Life of our life." And a very small number of our congregations, mostly in New England, were decidedly protestant Christian Unitarians, with Jesus and capital G God present every Sunday in scripture reading and pulpit theology.

And also during this time, as our UUA Principles and Purposes were being revised, our seminaries were studying the significance of the word *covenant* for a supposedly non-creedal set of congregations like ours. The revision of the Principles and Purposes in the 1980s brought this question to the fore. When I arrived to serve at Columbus, Ohio, the congregation had ordained a group of members to prepare words to describe the covenant we made with each other as a Unitarian Universalist congregation. They had once recited such words in the past, but there had been objections to some of the words, so no words were used for a while in worship. The commission presented the results of their hard work to the congregation at an annual meeting. The majority voted down the words and wanted to have no written covenant. The members of the commission were not happy, and I was more than a bit upset. Without a covenant to journey together in all our diversity while maintaining community, our congregation was out of step with our entire Unitarian Universalist history. And I said so one Sunday very candidly.

I decided to let things just stay that way, for all of us to simmer down, but each year, I myself would write what I called an "affirmation" for unison recitation in worship, which offered some idea to newcomers as to why we were there at all, and what gave us *distinction* as a congregation that called itself a *church.* For instance,

> And so, bearing witness *both* to our world as it is, *and* as Love can imagine it, we would claim that vision of a just world in our own lives as a summons to mission. And because of a growing sense of kinship with all beings, inviting our compassion, we begin in this celebration to engage our mission with our whole lives: body, mind, and heart.

I wrote these each year having entered into conversation with members about what the congregation meant to them, theologically and socially, and what they saw as its place in the world. I did this informally to get easy real answers without anyone thinking they were taking a quiz with "correct" answers. Then I made notes and wrote creatively from them.

Each year, the words were memorized by some people; and sometimes it was sad for me to let them go at year's end, because they often grew deeper in meaning for me and others as time went by.

But I agreed to no *final* words forever and ever. Amen.

And so the words were refreshed every year, unlike the credo of my youth, which has been recited for centuries, and unlike the "Love is the doctrine" and "Love is the spirit" covenants, which have lasted for decades. Both recited creed and written covenants of long duration become more unitive sounds of "this is what we do" traditions of local identity than fleshed out reasons why we gather at all. Recently, mission statements have taken on the role of covenant statements in some congregations. And longer, but not recited, "Covenants of Mutual Relations" have been added to congregational self-understanding of limits and boundaries on behavior in their communities.

And now the Principles have been replaced, four decades after they were last revised, in a world seething with divisions and spite that might have shocked the people crafting them.

The recent proposal to revise Article II surprised me at first, mostly because it appears to be a graceful geometric drawing rather than a progressive sequence of sentences.

Once I took that in stride, I read it through. All of the words are singular now. No one is trying to define them once and for all in tight sentences trying to stuff everyone's personal nuances and feelings into them.

And at the center is Love.

What to do with such a word that can be used in literally a million ways? For many, the word *love* has the resonances of Hallmark films, romance, and interpersonal chemistry. But bell hooks regards love as something far less tame. "The practice of love," she writes, "offers no place of safety. We risk loss, hurt, pain. We risk being acted upon by forces outside our control."[1]

The use of the single word Love at the center of the other words of principle invites what to me is a radical shift in our understanding of beloved community. Recitation is no longer an option. The word unadorned invites conversation and actions that elicit its deepest meaning *in community*. Our personal stories will of necessity become a spiritual discipline to share with each other in one way or another.

Creative co-ministerial work will create ways to engage the talkers and the non-talkers, the extroverts and introverts. There will be no one process and it will have to change over the years. It will invite fresh preaching and worship to help make this covenant vital and alive, and not just left on a shelf.

I'd like to conclude with questions written by my friend Dr. Michael J. Morris. They strike me as useful in approaching Love as the central Principle of our Association.

---

[1] bell hooks, *All About Love: New Visions* (Harper Perennial, 2001).

Who taught you about love? When and how have you felt you were loved? When and how have you felt you were loving? How did you know? How? How? When and how have you failed to be loving? And what will you do now differently? When and how have you *failed* to be loving—and what will you do now differently.

22

Love Is the Heart of This Church

Dan McKanan

"Love is the heart of this church." These are the first words in the covenant that my congregation, the Unitarian Universalist Congregation of Medford, Massachusetts, created several years ago. We say these words each Sunday to remind ourselves of who we are and of the promises we have made to one another. Our covenant invites us to see our diversity, our mutual support, and our work for justice as expressions of the love that beats at the heart of our community.

Those opening words echo the covenant crafted by Universalist L. Griswold Williams in the 1930s, and Williams's "Love is the doctrine of this church" is in turn an echo of "Love is the spirit of this church," from Unitarian James Vila Blake's 1884 covenant.[1] Our congregation used the Williams covenant for many years before writing our own, and the opening was the one part we opted to preserve. To ensure that everyone knows that we deliberately choose to put love first, we often introduce the covenant by saying, "Please join us in reciting our covenant, which begins with . . . ."

The Medford congregation's choice to put love first when talking about our shared values reflects a growing consensus among Unitarian Universalists. More and more, when we are

[1] L. Griswold Williams (#471) and James Vila Blake (#473) in *Singing the Living Tradition* (Beacon, 1993); Alison Cornish and Jackie Clement, "Leader Resource 1: A History of Covenant," in *Faith Like a River: Themes from Unitarian Universalist History* (Unitarian Universalist Association, 2011), uua.org/tapestry.

asked to distinguish the "transient" from the "permanent" elements in our tradition, love tops the list of items that still feel permanent.[2] And now we have made it official in the new "Purposes and Covenant" of the Unitarian Universalist Association. Love has both the last word in our statement of "purposes" and the first word in our list of values. We describe our common purpose as "the transformation of the world through liberating Love." We also affirm that

> Love is the power that holds us together and is at the center of our shared values. We are accountable to one another for doing the work of living our shared values through the spiritual discipline of Love.

These words do not constitute a new (or an old!) Unitarian Universalist "theology," for the ongoing work of theology can never be encapsulated in a single formula, no matter how carefully constructed.[3] Instead, the new Article II is an invitation to theolog*izing*, as individuals and communities dream up what it means to put love at the center. UU theologians of today and tomorrow—by which I mean all of us!—might well begin this work by wrestling with some of the questions that are stirred up by our new language.

We might ask, for example, whether the love we are talking about is a feeling or a way of acting? If love is the heart of this church, does that mean we should take a cue from our evangelical neighbors and use worship services to stir up intense, transformative emotions? Anyone who has attended a General

---

[2] Theodore Parker discussed the "transient and the permanent" in "The Transient and Permanent in Christianity," in Dan McKanan et al., eds., *A Documentary History of Unitarian Universalism*, Vol. 1 (Skinner House, 2017).

[3] This is true even for traditions that use binding creeds and covenants: the work of theology in those traditions is to keep the creedal teaching fresh by connecting it to the ever-changing life of the world.

Assembly worship service knows that many of us are yearning for more love-filled worship. But other Unitarian Universalists might respond by saying actions are more important than feelings and that love is real only when it is embodied in acts of service.

Other theologians will be tempted to recall that the ancient Greeks had three or four different words that correspond to the English word *love.* A lot of Christian theologians think that the really important love is agape—selfless, self-giving love, as exemplified by Jesus' death on the cross. But feminist theologians have argued that a focus on self-giving love is too one-sided. They say that we should pay more attention to eros, referring not only to sexual love but to all forms of love that are embodied and mutually beneficial. Love is most real when all the lovers feel more alive and connected.

Still others will ask, to *whom* is the love directed? Is the love at the heart of our church intended mostly for those of us inside our four walls, or should it extend out to the entire world? Unitarian Universalists talk a lot about "beloved community," but we haven't always been clear about whether this refers to the love and connection we feel when we are together or to the sort of society we hope to build alongside our neighbors of other faiths.

Each of these questions could inspire many books of theology. But the question that interests me the most is a bit different. When I read the new Article II, I wonder, who is doing the loving? When we say, love is the heart of this church, are we saying, this church is the place where *we* practice love? Or are we also saying that this is the place we go to find love? If we are saying that, where does the love come from? Does it just come from the other members of the church, or from something bigger than any of us?

This was one of the big questions that Unitarians and Universalists didn't manage to resolve when they merged sixty years ago and wrote the first version of Article II.

Historically, the two traditions had different "love languages." When Universalists talked about love, they meant God's love for humanity, or, in more inclusive language, cosmic love as one of the building blocks of reality. When Unitarians talked about love, they referred to the *human* duty to express love to God, other people, and the world. And when Unitarians and Universalists came together, they kept only the Unitarian version of love in Article II.

Specifically, they declared that one of their six Principles was "to cherish and spread the universal truths taught by the great prophets and teachers of humanity in every age and tradition, immemorially summarized in the Judeo-Christian tradition heritage as love to God and love to man."[4]

That passage reminds us of why it is sometimes important to change the language of our Principles! The use of *man* instead of *humanity* is an example of the sexist language that prompted Unitarian Universalists to rewrite Article II back in 1985. The phrase *Judeo-Christian* fails to honor the real differences between Judaism and Christianity. Lots of Jews and Christians would likely protest that "love to God and love to man" doesn't do justice to the complexity of their faiths. Though the phrase sounds generic, it was popularized by nineteenth-century Unitarians who were trying to make room for Transcendentalism and other post-Christian spiritualities. This was a time when Unitarians often found common cause with reform Jews, especially around their shared commitment to the social justice ideals of the Hebrew prophets.

"Love to God and love to man" also embodied Unitarian enthusiasm for the social gospel movement of the early twentieth century. Social gospelers taught that the Christian message of salvation was intended not just for individuals, but

[4] "Constitution of the Unitarian Universalist Association," in Dan McKanan et al., eds., *A Documentary History of Unitarian Universalism*, Vol. 2 (Skinner House, 2017).

for society as a whole. For them, Christianity was a "law of love." God's command to "love your neighbor as yourself" meant passing labor laws so that your neighbor would earn enough to feed their family and their children could go to school rather than having to work in a sweatshop. It meant working for peace and for an end to racial segregation. More recently, Cornel West has summed up the social gospel understanding of love in his declaration that "justice is what love looks like in public."[5]

Unitarian Universalists retained this social gospel view of love when they revised Article II in 1985. One big change at that time was that all references to our Christian roots were moved from the Principles to a brand-new list of Sources. As a result, the word *love* did not appear at all in the seven Principles of Unitarian Universalism. But it appeared in two of the six Sources. Source four gave a slightly more Universalist tilt to the original language: instead of "love to God and love to man," we had "Jewish and Christian teachings which call us to respond to God's love by loving our neighbors as ourselves." Source two doubled down on the social gospel vision by lifting up "words and deeds of prophetic women and men (since revised to *prophetic people*) which challenge us to confront powers and structures of evil with justice, compassion, and the transforming power of love."[6]

It would be a big stretch to say that the 1985 Principles and Sources put love at the center. But in the decades since, Unitarian Universalists have increasingly come to understand ourselves as "love people." Our enthusiasm for marriage equality is one expression of this. Another is the use of the phrase "side with love" to sum up our vision of social justice. As the Side with

---

[5] Cornel West, *Brother West: Living and Loving Out Loud, A Memoir* (Smiley, 2009).

[6] "The Principles and Purposes," in McKanan, *Documentary History*, 2.

Love website currently puts it, we "seek to harness love's power to stop oppression."[7]

The popularity of Side with Love is one of the main reasons that the Article II commission was charged to put love at the center of the new language. They took this charge seriously. They also retained the social gospel understanding of love as a human duty that must be manifested in social structures as well as interpersonal relationships. The new language affirms that love is a "liberating" power that we can use to "transform the world." It is also something that requires "discipline" and that holds us "accountable."

There is much to recommend this theology of love. Perhaps when we say that love is the heart of this church, what we mean is that this is a place where we take all the feelings of connection and caring that come naturally when we are with our family and friends and turn those feelings outward to embrace the whole world. This is not an easy task. It is not about sending Valentine's Day cards to the whole world. It is about doing the work of feeding the hungry, sheltering the homeless, and confronting those who serve power or greed rather than love. It is about doing the work of calling one another to account when we fall short of love's standard.

Disciplined and accountable love, rooted in both Unitarianism and the social gospel, is an important part of the love theology I wish to carry into the future. But it's not the *only* part, or even the most important part. If we put all the emphasis on our duty to love the world and on holding one another accountable, we imply that love starts with us. But it doesn't. We can love others only because we have first experienced love. I wish that we, as Unitarian Universalists, could tell a love story that begins long before our individual stories, and even before humanity's shared story. I want us to talk about love as part of the fabric of reality. When someone comes into our

[7] Side With Love, sidewithlove.org.

congregations, I'd like the first message they hear to be "You have always been loved." Only after they've really had a chance to take that in would I want them to hear the corollary, "You are accountable to love other beings."

"You have always been loved" was the core message of our Universalist predecessors, expressed first in theistic language and later in a more cosmic vocabulary. Across the centuries, the message was always the same: God is love. Love is God. Love will triumph over all. The Universalists' Winchester Profession affirmed, "We believe that there is one God, whose nature is Love."[8] Quillen Shinn, who planted dozens of Universalist congregations in the late nineteenth century, affirmed that "the force behind all forces and all worlds is love."[9] The social gospeler Clarence Skinner, who served one of our predecessor congregations during World War I, asserted that "The Universalist idea of God is that of a universal, impartial, immanent spirit whose nature is love. It is the largest thought the world has ever known."[10] For Universalists, human love was always in response to the love of the universe. "We believe in love," wrote one at the time of merger, "cosmic love as the creative force and human divine love as the law of life."[11]

Might such thoughts have a place in the Unitarian Universalist love theologies of the future? Many Unitarian Universalists could not, of course, affirm a Universalist theology of cosmic love if it were framed in theistic language. We might want love in the center, but we definitely want God off to the side, an option for some of us but not for all.

---

[8] "Profession of Faith," in McKanan, Documentary History, 1.

[9] Quillen Shinn, "Affirmations of Universalism," in McKanan, *Documentary History*, 2.

[10] Clarence Skinner, *Social Implications of Universalism*, in McKanan, *Documentary History*, 2.

[11] Albert Q. Perry, "The Uniqueness of Universalism," in McKanan, *Documentary History*, 2.

Personally, I am more comfortable with God language than many Unitarian Universalists, but even I am not comfortable with the way early Universalists understood God. Some early Universalists believed that a loving God would send everyone straight to heaven, regardless of how we behaved here on earth.[12] Even if I believed that were possible, it wouldn't appeal to me. It's too much like the Christianity I was brought up in, which taught that God loves us even though we are incapable of loving God. To me, that's not love. I don't want a God who loves me but doesn't care what I do. I want a God who loves me enough to help me become more loving.

I also cannot affirm the early Universalist faith that divine love is omnipotent, its victory guaranteed. If love were always victorious, we would have no racism, no war, no poverty, no mass extinction.[13] Even if we achieve a world without those things in the future, it wouldn't undo all the suffering of the present and the past.[14] To say that love is omnipotent, in the face of suffering, is to trivialize suffering and change the meaning of love beyond recognition.[15]

So if love is not all-powerful, what do I mean when I say that love is part of the fabric of reality? My answer builds on the work of theologians who call themselves religious naturalists, process theists, or pantheists, as well as holistic biologists and ecologists.

Through some mix of scientific observation and spiritual intuition, these thinkers affirm that every part of the universe

---

[12] Hosea Ballou and Edward Turner, "On Future Misery," in McKanan, *Documentary History*, 1.

[13] For a theological elaboration of this point, see William Jones, *Is God a White Racist? A Preamble to Black Theology*, rev. ed. (Beacon, 1997).

[14] Rebecca Parker and Rita Nakashima Brock, *Proverbs of Ashes: Violence, Redemptive Suffering, and the Search for What Saves Us* (Beacon, 2002).

[15] Charles Hartshorne, *Omnipotence and Other Theological Mistakes* (SUNY, 1984).

yearns for deeper relationship with every other part.[16] Neutrons and protons and electrons want to dance with one another and make atoms. Atoms seek each other out to make molecules. From the very beginning of life on earth, organisms found creative ways to connect. The earliest plants and animals were symbiotic communities of bacteria, each with a unique function that benefited the others.[17] Each new relationship unleashed new creativity, culminating in the beautiful, interdependent ecosystems of the world today. We can experience cosmic love in the beauty of a flower that has evolved to deepen the relationship between plant and pollinator.[18] In my own neighborhood, we can experience it in the persistence of the blueback herring, whose desire for the river leads them up passageways that have been blocked by dams for hundreds of generations. And we can experience it in what E. O. Wilson calls *biophilia*, or the desire of organisms to be in deep relationship with organisms of other species.[19] Biophilic love, of course, is what leads humans to remove the dams and let the herring swim free!

These examples should make it obvious that cosmic love is not all-powerful. Ecosystems can be disrupted. Humans, in fact any species, can get out of balance and destroy the other species in our community. If the second law of thermodynamics is

---

[16] Henry Nelson Wieman, *The Source of Human Good* (Southern Illinois University, 1946); Charles Hartshorne, *The Divine Relativity: A Social Conception of God* (Yale, 1982); Ursula Goodenough, *The Sacred Depths of Nature* (Oxford, 1998); Gordon Kaufman, *In the Beginning . . . Creativity* (Fortress, 2004); Catherine Keller, *On the Mystery: Discerning Divinity in Process* (Fortress, 2007); Carol Wayne White, *Black Lives and Sacred Humanity: Toward an African American Religious Naturalism* (Fordham, 2016); Jerome Stone, *Sacred Nature: The Environmental Potential of Religious Naturalism* (Routledge, 2017).

[17] Lynn Margulis, *Symbiotic Planet: A New Look at Evolution* (Basic, 1998).

[18] Robin Wall Kimmerer, *Braiding Sweetgrass: Indigenous Wisdom, Scientific Knowledge, and the Teaching of Plants* (Milkweed, 2013).

[19] Edward O. Wilson, *Biophilia: The Human Bond with Other Species*, rev. ed. (Harvard, 1984).

right, even love at the molecular level might eventually wear itself out.

But if love is not all-powerful, it is still, I think, the ultimate source of all the power we have. Love creates; hate destroys. Cities and gardens, forests and flowers, even our own beating hearts are made *of* love and *by* love. The love story began long before we were born, and it will continue long after we are gone.

So when I say, "Love is the heart of this church," I mean that I come to church to be reminded that I am part of the love story of the universe. I come to be embraced by the music we share every Sunday and enchanted by the flowers that we exchange during flower communion. I also come to join others in transforming the world with *our* liberating love. But that will be possible, I'm pretty sure, only if we first let ourselves be transformed by the world's liberating love.

23

Liberating Love

Rev. Fredric Muir

Several years before I completed three decades of ministry with a congregation of more than four hundred members, one of the longtime members asked me why the Unitarian Universalist Association was abandoning what had attracted him to our faith. Specifically, he thought that we were surrendering our historic legacy of inspiring values: "The religion I joined is being taken from me," he told an attentive audience at our annual meeting. Among those values were the Enlightenment-shaped trinity of freedom, reason, and tolerance expressed nowadays as individualism, affirming modernity, and the exceptionalist characterizing of our way of religion. I was surprised by his comments, but not alarmed; I'd heard versions of his concern from others.

***

Years before this event, theologian John Cobb wrote about the tension reflected in my congregant's question. Cobb frames the narrative of Enlightenment ideals:

> Today the limitations of Enlightenment modes of thought and of social organization are becoming more and more apparent. Whereas progress in the past two centuries has meant increasing the role of Enlightenment principles in our religious life, today it means something quite different. The dualism, the individualism, the rationalism,

> and the empiricism of the Enlightenment have all failed us . . . .[1]

It is important to say more about these guiding faith principles. The individualism that Cobb speaks of is an Enlightenment value that is an attracting and sustaining one for many Unitarian Universalists; it is also a value held sacred in American culture. Individualism is inscribed in our nation's foundational document as the right to pursue "life, liberty and the pursuit of happiness." Our Transcendentalist forebears recognized these as gifts from a loving God, shaping every person's uniqueness and reflecting in us the image of God. But it wasn't Transcendentalist individuality that drove settler occupation and genocide in the American West (supported by the tenets of Manifest Destiny) followed by imperial conquests of Pacific archipelagos (in which Unitarians and Universalists played outsized roles from 1893 to 1946). These hegemonic aspirations were activated by hyper-individualism rooted in entitlement, as in the right to use power over another because, well, because one could; most especially one could if he was a White Christian man. Over the decades, Transcendentalism's (Unitarianism) and a loving God's (Universalism) gifts-based individuality became so twisted and inflated that many express their understanding of Unitarian Universalism as a rights-based religion that gives you freedom to believe anything you want. We have become the iChurch.[2] While some have realized not just the shortcomings of the iChurch, but its mischaracterization of Unitarian Universalism, rights-based individualism remains strong in our congregations and a cherished principle in our nation's civil religion.

---

[1] John Cobb, "As Others See Us: Ecumenical Perspectives on Unitarian Universalism," *The Unitarian Universalist Christian* (Winter 1987).

[2] Fredric Muir, "The end of iChurch: To build Beloved Community, Unitarian Universalism needs a new narrative," *UU World* (Winter 2012), uuworld.org.

Consider another Enlightenment principle: Progressive religion in general and Unitarian Universalism in particular are eager to incorporate new ways of thinking. For example, the use of reason freed us from orthodox, literal reading of sacred scripture; reason opened us to modernity. But there have been times when we have been seduced by modernity, rushing to science for answers that faith didn't satisfy. One glaring example of this pivot away from a more cautious approach began as early as 1905, when Unitarian and Universalist laity, clergy, and their national organizations turned to eugenics as a way to sanction everything from colonization of BIPOC people to keeping a healthy home, from immigration restriction to juvenile individuation, from forced sterilization to church school curriculum development, from peace advocacy to publishing white supremacist authors. What is surprising is not that Unitarians and Universalists were among eugenics supporters; after all, we cast ourselves as a modern religion and eugenics was the epitome of modernity, but that given our size, the interest and support we showed was disproportionately large.

Combined with our version of individualism, embracing modernity shaped one more Enlightenment value, hubris. There should be little doubt as to how and why hubris is a shaping factor for Unitarian Universalists to address: Our Enlightenment principles put white, educated Unitarian Universalists on a pedestal; humility simply was never a significant part of our theology (nor is it today). Not that it couldn't be, but there has rarely been much/any consideration of it, which is to say that twenty-first-century Unitarian Universalism remains held in a faith posture shaped by exceptionalism.

* * *

The centuries "of progress" informed by these Enlightenment principles included our nation's era of imperialism from 1893 (when the Hawai'ian monarchy was overthrown) to deep into the twentieth century (while the Philippines was given independence in 1946, Puerto Rico and Guam remain unincorporated territories of the US). How these principles informed Unitarian and Universalist support and leadership in the colonization of Pacific island nations, including justifications from the American eugenics movement, remains an unspoken history in our Association and raises a question relevant for Unitarian Universalists: Are the Enlightenment principles and values that informed Unitarian Universalist support of the imperial era still shaping us, and if so, how? John Cobb believed they do and concluded:

> Can Unitarian Universalists find the resources to criticize the principles by which they have lived? If Unitarian Universalists could become self-critical in this way, you [Unitarian Universalists] could once again be in the vanguard of dealing with the most important issues of our time. I do not expect this, but I hope for it.

Article II in our Association's Bylaws calls us to "heal historic injustices" and on the Unitarian Universalist Association to "actively engage its members in the transformation of the world through liberating Love." It further states that "Love is the power that holds us together and is at the center of our shared values." What does this love look and feel like? How might it motivate and help us address and heal the brokenness resulting from our history of injustices, especially during our nation's imperial era? Is our imperial past still shaping us?

There appears to be no institutional legacy of love for us to reference, no sustained theological declaration of love and its transforming, liberating nature to guide us: While expressions about the power of love can be found in progressive religious writers and clergy, in few if any Unitarian or Universalist corporate documents has the singularity of love been named as a core value informing every aspect of our living tradition, as a binding inspiration or aspiration. This is important and should not be overlooked: The insertion and centrality of "love" in the recently approved Article II marks a significant shift for our Association and requires further reflection. There are two interdependent defining qualities of love that inform Article II and this essay, qualities that support post-Enlightenment definition and opportunities.

Love is hope. Our Transcendentalist ancestors bequeathed us theological imagination, the idea that the future's promise is always aspirational is foundational to hope. But imagination, while necessary, is not enough alone. Yara González-Justiniano notes several additional features of hope:

> *Solidarity* and *compassion* are key elements that require us to understand ourselves in relationship to others . . . . *Collective Work* generates a sustainable and liberative hope.[3]

Love is hospitality, which, like hope, is more than a Sunday morning expression or program. Hospitality is a posture, a way of being in the world. Radical welcoming will likely stretch many Unitarian Universalists who hold tightly to historic Enlightenment principles and values, which can have a narrowing and exclusionary nature. Peter Choi suggests that we might want to be "skeptical of aspirational language that enables us to preserve the status quo."[4] For example, some of us, in our eagerness to gift others with our unique way of religion, don't pause long enough to be mindful that radical hospitality also means receiving the gift of the other as they are (and not as we wish them to be), open to the way this gift might broaden and deepen us. Love as hospitality calls us to more than intellectual freedom, sharpened skills of reason, or willingness to tolerate

---

[3] Yara González-Justiniano, *Centering Hope as a Sustainable Decolonial Practice: Esperanza en Práctica* (Lexington, 2022).
[4] Peter Choi, "Deconstructed, reimagined faith," *Christian Century* (June 2023), christiancentury.org.

another's views. Love is about trust, care, and respect; love is about possibility. Love is radical hospitality, and welcome is receiving the gift of another as they are. Thank goodness there is encouraging support for those seeking a new path in the report of the Unitarian Universalist Association's Commission on Institutional Change.[5]

***

Peter Choi helped me understand why, at this time, love is central to our proposed purpose and covenant. There is a broader context to our consideration that is also shaping other faith communities. The COVID pandemic caused widespread suffering and exposed long-standing and ignored marginalizations. This combined with the rise of authoritarianism and the spread of war have led Choi to conclude, "As we come to understand more deeply the histories of empire, race, and slavery, turning away from triumphalism and toward lament feels like an appropriate spiritual response."

As with lament, the value of centering also occurs in stepping back from theological exceptionalism to honoring shared curiosity. Choi warns us that exceptionalism might be felt by others as "perilously indistinguishable from theological supremacy and its close kin White supremacy."

Finally, as we learn about the shortcomings and dangers of Enlightenment certitude, we embrace the power of mystery, the power of Love, as a priority. Choi remarks, "Certitude is not faith, many are realizing, and the dogmatic imposition of a debatable interpretation is not love."

These shifts illustrate a theo-ecclesial backstory to the centering of love in Article II, and understanding them encourages us to understand in their fullness the expectations

---

[5] Commission on Institutional Change, "Hospitality and Inclusion," *Widening the Circle of Concern* (Unitarian Universalist Association, 2020), uua.org/uuagovernance/committees/cic/widening/hospitality-inclusion.

and call that come with naming a foundation of love. Borrowing the words of Rabbi Danya Ruttenberg,

> The work of [love] demands curiosity, care, and a willingness to face hard things with bravery and honesty. While we can't undo the past, we can address the present with integrity and endeavor to create a future that is much more whole than anything we can imagine from here. So let us begin.[6]

***

To begin again in love requires, at the very least, a reckoning with the chaos and perils posed by Enlightenment principles. As congregations, organizations, and members learn about the ways their Unitarian/Universalist forebears and communities leveraged our faith to support our nation's imperial era (and other injustices), we must ask, *What now?*:

- Do the imperial mind and its shaping ideas still inform our Unitarian Universalist theology, our organizations, and our curricula?
- How can we—as individuals, as a congregation, as the denomination—speak truthfully about our past and then move forward on the foundation of love?
- In what ways are Enlightenment principles seemingly baked into our faith and holding us back from "the transformation of the world"?
- How can we live into a future shaped by the aspirational language in Article II?

With the spirit of *tikkun olam* (Hebrew for "repairing the world" and connoting social action and the pursuit of social

---

[6] Danya Ruttenberg, *On Repentance and Repair: Making Amends in an Unapologetic World* (Beacon, 2022).

justice), I propose a mnemonic that reflects our intention and offers a way forward: GO REPAIR[7]:

Gather a team that is representative of your organization (as it is and what it aspires to be, which may mean partnering with the larger community). If you are following this process as an individual, family, small group, you will likely need to adapt this first step (and others) to fit your size and purpose. Consider composing a mission statement. One of the goals of a mission statement is team clarity and transparency. If you are unfamiliar with mission statements and how to compose one, here is a place to start.[8]

Organize your team so everyone understands the purpose, expectations, and likely assignments. A covenant might help, since the team will work together to live into its mission and might need guardrails. A covenant is composed of promises expected from others and promises made. If you are new to covenants, consider using the Unitarian Universalist Association's workshop on writing a covenant.[9]

Remember to keep your stakeholders informed; part of your task may be unearthing secrets, so there's a danger of your team appearing to keep secrets yourselves, sending the unintentional message that you are continuing a perceived or real legacy of opaqueness. Remember to share the team's mission statement and covenant; transparency with leaders and stakeholders is critical, one way to earn trust and sustain integrity.

Research the context and actions around the topic. For example, what was going on—in your family, community, state, region,

---

[7] A longer version of the GO REPAIR device/process is included in my article "Seduced By the Sound of Science: Unitarians and Universalism in the Eugenics Era," *The Journal of Unitarian Universalist Studies*, Vol. XLV (2022).
[8] Douglas Zelinski, "Mission Statement Tips," *Leader Lab*, uua.org/leaderlab/mission-statement-tips.
[9] "Writing a Covenant Workshop," Unitarian Universalist Association, uua.org/safe/handbook/workshops/166375.shtml.

nation, the world—that might have given shape to the topic or event you are addressing?

Explore beyond the traditional research sites, which might involve a field trip and/or workshop/webinar, not just for one person but for the whole team. Think broadly and deeply. For example, recording interviews with those who might hold shaping information requires the interviewer to create a context free of fear, anxiety, blame, or guilt. Those who share their stories must feel confident that the interviewer and the team will present their words accurately. Here are some suggestions for doing interviews.[10]

Personalize the topic. This is a story that likely has a cast of players: individuals, families, institutions. Who were they, where were they from, where did they go? What were their personalities, backgrounds, and motivations? Where was the power coming from and going? Was power shared? Dig deep to look at how concepts and identities were created and how relationships were shaped. Are these still shaping your members, leaders, and organization?

Action to be taken could involve several steps, including a report to your stakeholders, a news article, and contact with others affected by the issue(s) you are naming. A word of caution: any action taken needs contextual thinking. Depending on the action, consider all the possible outcomes and people. Speaking truth to power is important, and so is care for those who have not lived up to their aspirations.

Incarnate your learnings with a deepening spiritual experience or exercise. A painting, sculpture, song, litany as a vehicle giving expression to the work, revelations, and feelings. This is

---

[10] "How to Do Oral History," *Smithsonian Institution Archives,* siarchives.si.edu/history/how-do-oral-history.

an opportunity for the team to partner with others and explore how the learnings become lessons resulting in a way forward.

Renew your purpose and aspiration after your group accepts the team's report. Plan for what difference your findings and reflections might make.

***

Article II states, "The Unitarian Universalist Association will actively engage its members in the transformation of the world through *liberating Love*" (emphasis added). The GO REPAIR exercise can offer support and clarity for an individual or group seeking change. Yet we don't know exactly what the composers of Article II meant by "liberating Love" or how they imagined it becoming an integrated and vibrant part of Unitarian Universalism. I hope this essay has helped give depth to their intention. And there are at least three compelling understandings I can add to the theo-cultural foundation erected on this Love.

First is "liberating Love" as an expression or phrase that reminds and holds us accountable to an aspiring religious tradition and future. We Unitarian Universalists don't have many commonly held expressions of this kind, of a kind with theological, spiritual, and ecclesial consensus. Now, with the language of Article II, we might hold up the phrase "liberating Love" as uniquely our own (in the same way as "Side With Love"): We are the faith community who seeks to transform the world with liberating Love!

Another understanding reflects the history I alluded to earlier, that there has never been a Unitarian/Universalist corporate statement that places Love at the center of our religion. In this way, it's as though we have held Love captive and now arrived at a time to liberate Love. In this way, "Liberating Love" is a freeing action, releasing what has been held back, out of view for decades (centuries?). Moving forward with a liberated and liberating Love, we might even have a sense of being refreshed when inspired and energized by the transforming power of Love.

Finally, as a phrase or as a statement of intent, "liberating Love" could mean transforming ourselves. The GO REPAIR process is one way (but certainly not the only way) to give "liberating Love" direction. To what end? Rabbi Ruttenberg asserts, "Addressing harm is possible only when we bravely face the gap between the story we tell about ourselves . . . and the reality of our actions . . . even if it threatens our story of ourselves." And especially for those of us living with the love language of Article II: "Taking seriously that I might have hurt you is an act of love and care. It is an opportunity to open my heart wider than it has been . . . to let your experience matter."

* * *

In 1936, the American Unitarian Association's (AUA) newly established Commission of Appraisal issued its first report (a hefty book of 350 pages), *Unitarians Face a New Age*. In the report's first section, "Introduction: Re-Thinking Unitarianism," they set the tone of their findings with a strong, frame-bending warning:

> The genius of the Unitarian movement has been its power to adapt the vocabulary and practices of a religion whose roots are sunk deep into the past to new knowledge, new conditions, and new situations. If this genius should fail us now, the time will have come to write 'finis' to the story of Unitarianism.[11]

[11] Commission of Appraisal, *Unitarians Face a New Age* (American Unitarian Association, 1936).

While the Commission's bold and sobering words are appropriate for any discussion about the future of Unitarian Universalism, in 1936 they were unaware of, oblivious to, ignoring, didn't care about, or maybe agreed with the several ways their leaders (and ancestors) leveraged their faith to support imperialism in its many hegemonic directions. The Commission reported six values with which Unitarians agreed; the value of love is not named and the absence of a theology of love or even language about love is conspicuous. Perhaps the AUA's commitment to Enlightenment principles and values left no room for naming the centrality of love. Now it feels important to ask: Might the absence of love—especially as hope and hospitality—have been a contributing factor shaping the Commission's deep concern regarding the future of our way of religion? Is it time now not only to pay close attention to this absence, but to correct it?

We recall that our Universalist tradition speaks of a God who unconditionally affirms and loves all, a faith stance rejected by many religious conservatives. Broadening his understanding of Love, Universalist minister Hosea Ballou remarked,

> If we agree in brotherly love, there is no disagreement that can do us any injury; but if we do not no other agreement can do us any good.[12]

As bold as Ballou's words might have been—and still may be—they fall short of what we need today. In many of our settings, we need a love that moves beyond agreement and disagreement. Article II states, "We are accountable to one another for doing the work of living our shared values through the spiritual discipline of Love." This requires a love that supports and challenges us, claims yet pushes us, centers and moves us. With a love shaped by imagination, hope, and hospitality, we can make real the promises that are ours to keep.

[12] Hosea Ballou, *A Treatise on Atonement* (1848).

24

Finding Love in the Streets

Rev. Jason Lydon

In November of 2001, I found myself in a van owned by the Unitarian Universalist Association driving through the night with a group of youth who were part of the Young Religious Unitarian Universalist (YRUU) movement. We headed from Massachusetts to Columbus, Georgia. The previous summer, YRUUers and members of the Continental Unitarian Universalist Young Adult Network (C*UUYAN) affirmed our ongoing collaborative efforts. We were living amid the anti-globalization movement, and our youth and young adult visions of justice called upon us to take action. Workshop after workshop taught us that global capitalism was incompatible with our Unitarian Universalist values. We were learning about the harms of white supremacy culture and engaging in visionary discussions about what a liberated world rooted in love would look like. A world that centered love at its core would be so different from the one we inherited.

At General Assembly, it was decided that we would gather youth and young adults to raise our voices together, joining the interfaith movement to shut down the US Army School of the Americas (SOA, since renamed the Western Hemisphere Institute for Security Cooperation). For years, protesters gathered at the entrance of Fort Benning, where the SOA was based. Thousands upon thousands rallied for an end to the state violence embodied in SOA practices. In 1998, our own faith movement passed an Action of Immediate Witness calling for the immediate closure of the SOA and an investigation into the countless human rights abuses graduates of the SOA perpetrated in Latin America. While Unitarian Universalists were a powerful force in the movement to close the SOA, it was truly a movement rooted in the radical Catholic tradition.

For me, the Catholic Worker Movement offers a powerful lesson in love. Co-founder Dorothy Day wrote,

> If we love enough, we are going to light a fire in the hearts of others . . . . It is love that will make us want to do great things for each other. No sacrifice and no suffering will then seem too much.[1]

Protesting the SOA required little sacrifice and suffering of most protesters, though there is risk any time one gathers in the streets in the name of justice. The annual SOA protest lasted through the weekend. Friday night, people gathered for an evening of workshops and documentaries. Saturday, protesters rallied outside the military base and listened to speakers, including labor organizers from Colombia, religious leaders from El Salvador, Indigenous environmental justice freedom fighters from Mexico. Saturday night, many would gather and discuss the tactics of civil disobedience to be employed the following day in a symbolic action of trespassing on the military base. Sunday was the most meaningful part of the weekend action. On this day, protesters gathered in a solemn procession as names of those murdered by graduates of the SOA were read aloud, and the protesters responded with a collective chorus, "presente." Many of us could feel the present spirit of those whose lives had been stolen by graduates of the SOA. Collective power, action, and shared grief illuminated the power of love burning brightly in the hearts of those gathered.

I learned about radical love in the streets. Protesting the SOA was one part of a larger movement that envisioned a

---

[1] Robert Ellsberg, ed., *Dorothy Day: Selected Writings* (Orbis, 2005).

global community rooted in collective power from the bottom up as opposed to a global capitalism that exploited billions worldwide, creating devastation from the top-down. Across national and global protests, I found the truth of love echoing loudly in the streets. I learned about radical love at the World Economic Forum protest, the World Trade Organization protest, the World Bank protest, the International Monetary Fund protest, and the life transforming anti-Iraq war protests. I found love in a mass of beautiful protesters, listening to the voices of grassroots organizers, chanting and crying, promising to build a voice of resistance even in the face of overwhelming violence. This was where I found a radical love that refused to allow our imagination of a just world to be squashed. This is where I found the transformative power of collective love, the *agape* love Dr. King proclaimed over and over again.

It is necessary to clarify what is meant by *radical love*. For me, radical love is creative, visionary, and relational. In the justice context, this love is not simply antagonistic, anti-this and anti-that. Radical love requires a deep longing for the betterment not just of humanity, but of the world we belong to and with an understanding of our connectedness through the entirety of the universe.

Dr. Dana Stachowiak of the Educator Collaborative writes,

> Radical love is love amplified. It's love with a double shot of social justice. Paulo Freire's vision of radical love is one that is 'never about absolute consensus, or unconditional acceptance, or unnecessary words of sweetness . . . . instead, it is unconstructed, rooted in a committed willingness to struggle persistently with purpose in our life . . . to be lively, forceful, and inspiring,

while challenging and insistent . . . and intimately connected to what it means to "be human."[2]

Radical love isn't about violence and silence; it is about peace and action. It's about courage, not fear, and it is about a commitment to others. If you centered this vision of radical love in your life, how might it change your behavior?

I connect deeply with Freire's vision of radical love. I saw that vision in action in the streets of cities across the country where I learned of "lively, forceful, and inspiring" love. I will never forget marching against the war in Iraq with tens of thousands of people gathered in Washington. On one march, I found myself with friends and fellow organizers from the University of Massachusetts, many of us members of the Radical Student Union. We organized on campus, building a collective student voice for peace with justice. In our learning, we expanded our understanding of state violence beyond war to include police. We had experienced militarized police forces at protests when they came out in tanks and riot gear, with chemical warfare, attacking and suppressing anyone expressing dissent.

Of course, there has always been violence in policing. Historically, police forces were designed to enforce oppression, and the more we understood that, the more we realized opposing war would not be sufficient in our work to center love and liberation. We would be called to oppose all state violence, including that perpetrated by the police. During the unforgettable march in Washington, I found myself with a group of other students wrapping our arms around the body of another young protester who the police had picked off. Two of us took the person's arms and another two took their torso, and we just yanked and pulled, twisted and turned until the person was free. They ran off after being freed, and we did the same.

---

[2] Dana Stachowiak, "Living, Breathing, and Teaching with Radical Love: What It Means, What You Need, and Where to Start," *The Educator Collaborative*, community.theeducatorcollaborative.com.

There was no need to say, "Thank you." There was no need to say, "You're welcome." This was love in action. This was protecting one another. This was lively, forceful, and inspiring love.

Unitarian Universalists commonly sing one of my favorite hymns: "When I breathe in, I breathe in peace. When I breathe out, I breathe out love."[3] I can hear the music in my head anytime I read the words. I love the descant, the counter melody, just as much as I love the drone part, "Breathe in. Breathe out." The song creates a beauty that moves me to tears. Breathing out love cultivates a sense that we have love within ourselves that can be shared with those around us. Within you, within your neighbor, within me—we all have a blessing of love that we get to spread with great joy. I wonder, though, can we also breathe out righteous anger along with love? Can we be so angry at the world's injustices and yet breathe out love?

Or is it possible that our anger is fueled by our radical love? Beverly W. Harrison writes,

> Anger is not the opposite of love. It is better understood as a feeling-signal that all is not well in our relation to other persons or groups or to the world around us . . . . anger signals something amiss in relationship . . . . Such anger is a signal that change is called for, that transformation in relations is required.[4]

Change is needed, and love just may help us get there. Change is needed, and anger may just show us which brokenness we must attend to most urgently. Transformation is needed; love and anger can guide us along a path of righteousness. Is this what it may mean to center love in our faith?

---

[3] Sarah Dan Jones, "When I Breathe In," *Singing the Journey* (Unitarian Universalist Association, 2005), #1009.

[4] Beverly W. Harrison, "The Power of Anger in the Work of Love" in *Union Seminary Quarterly Review*, Vol. XXXVI (1981).

Many Unitarian Universalists have found love in the streets, even if we don't explicitly label it as such. Thousands of Unitarian Universalists have taken to the streets, demanding an end to the pervasive anti-Black violence perpetrated by police nationwide. While individual instances of police murder have garnered specific attention, the widespread movements across the country underscored the devastating impact of police violence on Black communities everywhere, transcending isolated incidents in specific cities. Police often function as a tool of anti-Blackness. However, the protests we participated in were not solely centered on Black suffering, but also on loudly proclaiming "Black Lives Matter," articulating a profound love of Blackness and Black people, a love that vehemently refused to allow the perpetuation of state violence to go on without accountability.

Jordan Brown also writes of radical love. They urge readers to embrace a love that celebrates resistance and refuses to be hidden under a bushel. "My heritage," they write,

> is also one of radical love, a love that intentionally includes the most marginalized in our society instead of focusing on abstract, mollifying concepts like diversity and representation. For allies, radical love does not mean only sharing aesthetically pleasing graphics about anti-Black violence online or posting a pointless black square on your feed. Radical love means challenging anti-Blackness—including misogynoir, transmisogynoir, colorism and anti-Black ableism—wherever you encounter it, whether that be in your family, in your friend group, on your social media timeline or at protests.[5]

[5] Jordan Brown, "VIEWPOINT: Embrace Radical Love," *The Hoya* (June 23, 2020), thehoya.com.

As Unitarian Universalists, we highlight the need to center love in our theological framework, in our community framework, and in the covenant that defines relationships between congregations. The kind of love we move into the center matters. The love we need to center is not sentimental love (though sentimental love can be sweet and necessary). The love we need to center must, as Brown writes, be "a love that intentionally includes the most marginalized." Does the love you center include sex workers? Undocumented migrants? Drug users? Prisoners? Who is beyond your circle of love? Is it even possible, as Unitarian Universalists, for us to center love in our liberating faith if we do so without centering the most marginalized?

Liberation struggle cannot take place only on the streets. The love we need to center in these struggles crosses movements, crosses communities, crosses ideologies, crosses theologies. When we follow the leadership of the most marginalized we have a greater potential of finding liberation movements rooted in love. This following must resist tokenization, fetishizing, or valorizing marginalized communities. To center love in our work, our ministry, we must build authentic relationships and practice deep listening so that we can take big risks together.

I've spent most of my adult life involved in the penal abolition movement. This is a movement created and led by those who have been the targets of the carceral state for generations, particularly Black women and prisoners. The abolition movement believes we can live in a world free from police and prisons. Abolitionism is not a utopian dream; it is a practical movement striving for material changes to systems that deny life, particularly Black life. There have been three Unitarian Universalist Actions of Immediate Witness that include calls for the abolition of prisons and/or police. Of course, not all Unitarian Universalists are abolitionists, but these Actions mean that we have the power within our faith movement to embrace a radical love. Radical love empowers us to imagine not only that new worlds are possible, but that we are capable of the work to create them. Much like the movement to abolish chattel slavery, the present-day abolitionist movement is rooted in a belief that people are sacred and must not be held captive. It is a movement that believes explicitly that Black people deserve freedom, It is a movement that believes in love's power to transform the world through accountability and transformation rather than punishment and violent repression.

Creating systems of accountability for behavior is central to the work of abolition. In reality the vast majority of violence perpetrated by people in our society goes unpunished by the criminal legal system. The vast majority of people who sexually assault someone will never experience consequences. The countries, particularly the United States, that fund and support Israel's genocide of Gaza will likely experience no consequences. Bullies in school—no consequences. The list goes on. One of the most beautiful and powerful aspects of abolition is not in the call to dismantle, but rather in the call to build something new. In this new imagining, we find the roots of love. This love is not just for people who have experienced harm, but also for people who cause harm. The vision of accountability is not to punish "perpetrators" and to get "justice" for "victims." Instead, within the vision of transformative justice, accountability creates new systems that imagine radically different ways of engaging with peoples' behavior. Kai Cheng Thom writes,

> we must love ourselves. we must encourage love—love that is radical, love that digs deep. love that asks the hard questions, that is ready to listen to the whole story and keep loving anyway. love for the survivors, love for the perpetrators, love for the survivors who have perpetrated and the perpetrators who have survived. love for the community that has failed us all. we live in poison. the planet is dying. we can choose to

> consume each other or we can choose love. even in the midst of despair, there is always a choice. i hope we choose love.[1]

Abolition is a movement built on love and hope, love for people and hope for humanity. It has been said that people are able to believe in God with little evidence and that humanists are able to believe in humans despite endless evidence to the contrary. This is overly simplified and likely not affirmed by all theists who find evidence of God in so much of the universe's existence. What I do like about the adage, though, is the point that those of us who are humanists must maintain a deep sense of faith because humans teach us all the time that we can choose to embrace overwhelming harm when we could otherwise choose care, compassion, or, most importantly, love. Kai Cheng Thom is beseeching us to choose love. As Unitarian Universalists, we are making a conscious choice to center love if we adopt Article II.

I found love in the streets. Movements for justice teach us how to love fiercely. I have been blessed to find love arm-in-arm with Unitarian Universalists who know, as Arundhati Roy writes,

> Another world is not only possible, she is on her way. On a quiet day, I can hear her breathing.[2]

If we are to breathe in peace and breathe out love, we must transform the world we live in. Centering love in our faith is a bold and necessary choice. It is a proclamation that we will choose sides, not between certain peoples, but between that which is just and that which is not. We will use our voice, even when it is risky, because that is what love calls us to do. How we center love matters. Now is the time for us to define, redefine,

---

[1] Kai Cheng Thom, "I Hope We Choose Love: Notes on the Application of Justice," *Medium* (May 5, 2018), medium.com.
[2] Arundhati Roy, *War Talk* (South End, 2003).

and define again what we mean when we say "love." I choose to center a radical love—a love that promises to unarrest, promises to write prisoners' letters, promises to hold one another accountable for harm, promises to authentically listen, and promises to change. I found this radical love in the streets. Where do you?

25

Death and Glory, Love and Evil

Rev. Ashley Horan

> We can disagree and still love each other, unless your disagreement is rooted in my oppression and the denial of my humanity and my right to exist.
>
> —Robert Jones, Jr.

As a seventeen-year-old committed Unitarian Universalist attending a conservative, all-girls, Catholic high school, pop culture that reflected my theology was extremely rare. So when Kevin Smith released his 1999 religious satire *Dogma,* I was ecstatic. While the whole film was a vibe—crass, irreverent, deep, hilarious—it was the closing scene that shook my spirit (insert spoiler alert here for a twenty-five-year-old film that you can't even find on streaming platforms anymore):

Without going deeply into the convoluted plot, suffice it to say that at the end of the film, rogue angel Bartleby (*Tiger Beat* 90s heartthrob Ben Affleck) has gone on a murderous rampage and is about to bring about Armageddon, having trapped God in the body of a comatose human. At the last moment, the heroine (Linda Fiorentino) pulls the plug and God is released, immediately appearing before the unhinged angel in a new body (Alanis Morrissette, of course) to intervene. God gently approaches Bartleby, and they lock eyes; as he gazes into Her face, his expression melts from wrath to epiphany to remorse. "I'm so sorry," he sobs as God opens Her arms and cradles his head tenderly to Her chest. She steps back as Bartleby whispers,

"Thank you," closing his eyes and leaning back in a posture of openness. God opens Her mouth in a cataclysmic roar, and the angel's physical form explodes into shards of flesh and light as he is presumably reintegrated back into the cosmic heaven that welcomes us all after death.

It wasn't until a decade later, in my first UU history class in seminary, that I discovered theological language for this semi-tongue-in-cheek scene. In the early nineteenth century, I learned, the "Ultra Universalists" held that not only is God too loving to condemn anyone to eternal damnation, even the most unrepentant sinners will see God's face at the moment of death and be immediately cleansed of their wickedness, reconciled with God, and welcomed into heaven. These "Death-and-Glory Universalists," as their detractors snidely referred to them, engaged in fiery debates with the Restorationists, who believed that while God was magnanimous enough to eventually welcome all Their children into paradise, sinners must endure a period of purifying punishment (perhaps eons long) before they were "restored" to God's good graces.

In those early, earnest years of my ministerial formation, I wholeheartedly embraced a more metaphorical version of Ultra Universalism. As an abolitionist, I could never abide the idea of eternal punishment. And while I have never been a strong theist, I do believe that the Universe has embedded within it a will toward goodness and flourishing and love, and that every human innately has an inclination to align with that will. While systems of oppression and trauma dampen that impulse within us, leading people and communities to perpetrate harm, our inborn alignment with and belonging to Love can never be fully snuffed out. While there may not be a literal heaven awaiting us after death, once our spirits are no longer contorted by the wounds we have inherited and inflicted in this life, I believe we are subsumed into that moral arc of the universe that bends toward Love and Justice. More simply put, I agree with Bryan Stevenson's assertion that "each person is more than the worst thing they've ever done," and I trust that we are all held by an unshakable Love that will not let us go.

The most frequent argument against Universalism has always been that without the threat of eternal punishment, humans would have no compelling reason not to sin. Rooted in a Calvinist theology that pronounced all human souls blemished from birth by the taint of original sin, many Christians of the nineteenth century pushed back against the burgeoning Universalist movement in America by arguing that sinning was simply too enjoyable to give up if people weren't terrified by the notion of everlasting fire and brimstone.

But the Universalists argued that not only is God too good to forsake us, humans are hard-wired to act lovingly because we are created in the image of divine Love itself. The great eighteenth-century Universalist preacher and theologian Hosea Ballou wrote,

> God's moral law is like himself, love. "God is love, and he who loveth dwelleth in God and God in him." It requires all moral beings to love God and each other; and the reason why it commands this is, it is love itself. True, that soul is miserable that does not love God, and the reasons are, love is the life and happiness of the soul, and hatred is its death and misery.[1]

In other words, the human soul is innately attuned to Love's will for what is right and good, and thus loving is its own reward just as hating is its own punishment.

My own embodied experience tells me that Ballou's assertion that "love is the life and happiness of the soul" is true. For me, there is a physical sensation of Love that is fully in alignment with both the cellular level of my own being and the cosmic level of the universe. I think of the first exquisitely

[1] Hosea Ballou, A *Treatise on Atonement* (1848).

overwhelming moments when I held my newborn babies to my sweaty chest after they struggled through birth into this life; the breath hitch of awe I feel standing on a pine-covered outcropping overlooking an expanse of open wilderness water in the Northwoods; the pulsing energy of thousands of voices raised in song and chant during a march or a direct action, when change feels not only possible but unstoppable . . . . At these times, I feel what I can only describe as the physical equivalent of the sound made by a full orchestra playing the soaring final note of a glorious piece of music, when the frequencies of each of the instruments resonate in a harmony so perfect all those who can hear it transcend together. When I experience this full-body sensation of alignment with the frequencies of love, I find myself so clearly knowing, "This! This feeling! *This* is what I was made for; what we were *all* made for."

But what about the converse? Is hatred really the "death and misery" of the soul? I don't think of myself as a hateful person; I don't regularly wish or work intentionally for the harm of other people, and I have never committed an act of physical violence against another person. But if we understand *hate* or *sin* as feelings or actions toward other living beings that make it less possible for those beings to thrive and flourish, then I am as big a hateful sinner as any. Perhaps not so dramatically as when I physically feel that alignment with Love, but I do physically experience the jaggedness of *mis*alignment: the twinge in my stomach when I do my Christmas shopping on Amazon for budgetary reasons, knowing that my choices are likely contributing to everything from sweatshop labor to rising carbon emissions to union busting. The ache in my chest when I lose my temper at my beloved child and I can see them shrink into themselves at the harshness of my tone. The waves of nausea when someone I care about tells me directly that my behavior toward them has perpetuated classism or racism or ableism, and I have harmed them with my failure.

But I also know how easy it is to inure myself against these signals that some might call conscience; to make excuses for my behavior until the patterns are so ingrained that I've forgotten what it feels like to not repeat them. The discomfort of misalignment with Love—what Ballou calls "hatred" or "sin"—becomes an ever-present white noise in the background rather than an acute pain requiring my attention and intervention.

I can only believe that the same goes for all of us, including people whose ingrained patterns and repeated behaviors rise to the level of evil directed toward other beings. From the person who has convinced themself that their partner deserved that kick in the ribs; to the "Mom for Liberty" who truly believes that she is protecting her child when she advocates for racist, transphobic policies; to the "pro-life" activist who firebombs the abortion clinic to "save the unborn babies"; to the leaders of nations who insist that wiping "human animals" off the map is the only path to defending their own people, I believe that with enough repetition, we are all capable of developing a tolerance to misalignment with Love and justifying our behavior, no matter how heinous. Human history and our own lived experience contain innumerable examples that challenge the Ultra Universalists' assertion that the internal torture of hatred and sin are enough to prompt repentance, let alone deter us from doing evil in the first place.

In the more-than-fifteen years since I first learned that vocabulary, my rather abstract version of Death-and-Glory Universalism has been challenged again and again as I have encountered the depths of our human capacity for evil and have learned that many hearts and minds simply cannot be changed. I think of the night during my chaplaincy internship when I sat with a nineteen-year-old whose boyfriend had intentionally pushed her and her newborn down the stairs, causing the baby to fly through a plate-glass window to his death. Witnessing up close the hatred and contempt smoldering in the eyes of police as they aimed their tear gas and rubber bullets as we gathered in mass protest after the murders of Jamar Clark, Philando Castile, and George Floyd. Feeling the chill slither down my spine as I listen to any number of fascist politicians and media personalities speak with calm conviction about how everyone who isn't white, male, able-bodied, wealthy, and documented needs to be systematically controlled, criminalized, or eliminated. History shows that those who intentionally wield their power to dominate and degrade other humans are very unlikely to have a *sui generis* crisis of conscience and repent of their misdeeds.

My abolitionist ethic and Universalist theology are both core enough to who I am that I don't desire punishment for those who commit evil acts; I don't think it will bring more justice into the world if we imprison or torture or kill perpetrators of hatred and violence. But I do yearn for accountability; it absolutely irritates my soul to know that, in all likelihood, the Donald Trumps of the world are not only going to "get away with" their illegal and immoral acts, they are never going to have that moment of epiphany that gives way to remorse (at least, not in this lifetime). I also believe that precisely *because* humans are held by an unshakeable Love that yearns for our freedom and flourishing, we are never required to tolerate abuse or degradation from others. So what does it look like, especially on the mass scale, to "put Love at the center" not just in working with our allies, but in ongoing adversarial relationship with people who are literally trying to kill us?

In my fifteen years of experience organizing UU individuals, congregations, and organizations, we do fairly well at the former (i.e., we can sustain loving, covenantal relationship with people who are similar enough to us in identity and/or ideology that they do not pose significant threats to our worldview). Our people love to organize *for* voting rights, immigration access, abortion rights, LGBTQIA+ equity, and climate and racial justice. But Unitarian Universalists have a deep discomfort in unequivocally proclaiming that we are *against* anything, and we struggle mightily to directly name evil and look its perpetrators squarely in the face.

I have witnessed this reluctance many times in my UU organizing work, from facilitating congregational anti-racism trainings, to leading a UU state action network, to serving for the past four and a half years as the Unitarian Universalist Association's organizing strategy director, a position in which I have led the team that holds the outward-facing justice work of the Association under the banner of Side With Love (SWL). In the early days of SWL, for example, there were quite a few loud voices who protested that the campaign's name was "divisive" because it required "choosing sides" when we are a "pluralistic religion that shouldn't tell anyone what to believe." While exponentially more Unitarian Universalists were clear that our faith does indeed demand clarity and conviction on matters of justice, the undertone of unease about accepting that there is a moral imperative to name and counteract evil (even when that can be polarizing) has never entirely vanished.

During the height of the Black Lives Matter movement between 2014 and 2020, I heard more Unitarian Universalists than I care to count protesting that while they believed in racial justice, the agitational tactics of freeway shutdowns and the mass calls for abolishing policing and prisons were "inconsiderate," "too aggressive," and "outlandish." And "After all, doesn't our Universalism mean that *all* lives matter?"

During our first round of Side With Love's UU the Vote campaign in 2020, our Organizing Strategy Team led trainings to prepare congregations to show up skillfully in the event of mass uprising, disruption, and anti-democratic tactics (including violence) surrounding the national elections. We had relatively low attendance and heard frequently from both congregations and religious professionals that preparation for such "doomsday scenarios" was "alarmist" and "paranoid"—nothing like that could happen in the U.S. Many Unitarian

Universalists maintained that position up until (and in some cases long after) the January 6 attempted coup.

My theory is that contemporary Unitarian Universalists often fail to directly confront evil because we have largely embraced a watered-down version of Universalism that still struggles with the question "If we are all held by a Love that will never forsake us, and don't believe in a retributive afterlife, how can we reconcile our inborn belovedness with the depths of evil of which humans are capable?" I frequently think that the twenty-first-century liberal version of Ballou's formulation "Hate and misery are the death of the soul" is "They wouldn't believe [xyz heinous thing] if they only had all the facts." We obliquely reference "pluralism" and "nonviolence" as passive, overindulgent postures that enable violent systems and actors to persevere, rather than the rigorous, principled spiritual disciplines they should be. We stop at the Universalist assertion about the inherent worth and dignity of every person without acknowledging that honoring someone's inborn Belovedness absolutely means taking active measures to prevent them from impeding other people's access to freedom and flourishing.

And so Unitarian Universalists, like most liberal-to-progressive groups, shirk the kind of organizing and action that requires sustained, intimate interfacing with evil systems and their participants. We prefer an anonymous textbank to a deep canvassing conversation; we repost a pithy meme on socials but refrain from testifying at the City Council meeting or arguing with Uncle Bob; we refrain from protesting against brutality and genocide because it will upset our multifaith colleagues or our large donors.

It can be overwhelming, heartbreaking, even traumatizing, to fully reckon with the gravity of evil. At the time of writing this essay, for example, our faith and the international community continue to argue about whether the Israeli government's killing of more than 40 thousand Palestinians constitutes genocide. More than five hundred pieces of anti-trans legislation were introduced in the U.S. in 2023, and 25 states have severely restricted or entirely criminalized abortion. Texas Gov. Greg Abbott has trafficked more than 30 thousand migrants to Chicago in the past six months; Florida has passed legislation that prevents teaching about race, gender, and sexuality; and there is a very real chance that the 2024 election will pave the way for the U.S. to become a dictatorship.

In the face of these kinds of horrific acts, if we define Love as a nebulous warm feeling toward an individual or a group and then propose that we "center Love" in our organizing, we are doomed. If "Love thy enemy" is code for "swallow your feelings, don't confront, don't disturb, don't take sides, turn the other cheek even when they keep on slapping you (or your neighbor)," then not only will we suffer the indignities and trauma perpetrated by those who would do us harm, but we will also be aiding and abetting that same violence toward others—a sin in and of itself.

Universalism doesn't require us, individually, to love every other human; as I often quip, "That's God's job, way above my paygrade." But it does demand that we behave in ways that do not dehumanize or degrade our enemies, even as we actively resist them and strategically work toward a world in which all people can access the freedom and flourishing that Love wills for each and all of us.

The time is now for Unitarian Universalists to reinvent and reclaim a Universalism that is neither naive about the realities of evil nor retributive in its tactics against those who perpetrate it. Putting Love at the center of our faithful organizing means nurturing both the clarity to act boldly for the liberation and thriving of all people and the earth and the fortitude to name and confront violence and hatred at all levels. Our spiritual task must be to resist numbness, engaging evil directly so that we may combat it with strategy, skill, and resolve.

Simultaneously, we must also protect within ourselves the ability to resonate on that soul-deep level with the will of Love, so that we may consistently summon the courage to respond to its call. And that work is best done in community—in our daily efforts to extend tenderness to our beloveds; in our neighborhood associations, organizing collectives, and movements for justice; and in the pews each week, as we worship together and remind one another of the Love that is both our birthright and our calling.

26

Love Is a Circle in Time

Rev. Rebecca Ann Parker

In a small group gathering of Unitarian Universalist ministers many years ago, we were asked to respond to the question "What is at the center of Unitarian Universalism?" People offered a variety of answers: freedom of belief, covenant with one another, openness to new revelation, and more. Then the elder in our group spoke, a self-described "old-time Universalist" and we heard the voice of one long seasoned in ministry. "Our elders," he said, "used a phrase that expressed it." He silently opened his hands with a broad sweep, "And underneath are the everlasting arms." Something in the gentle force of how he spoke and the shining confidence in his eyes brought a hush over the group. For a moment, it was as if those arms had materialized and embraced us all—or so it seemed to me.

"Underneath are the everlasting arms" is from the Bible (Deuteronomy 33:27). Moses proclaims this as his final word to his people before his death, as he gazes from the mountaintop, across the Jordan to the "land flowing with milk and honey" that he will not live to see. As his people prepare to move forward on their journey without him, Moses tells them they face a choice: life or death, blessing or curse. He enumerates the grave curses their choice may engender—war, hunger, environmental devastation. He bestows the blessings to come if they choose the right path: abundance, peace, and security. "Choose life!" he urges. His final words of warning and encouragement look back to the painful years of enslavement in Egypt, the difficult flight to freedom, the struggle over false worship, the gift of miraculous sustenance in the long desert journey, the exhaustion of discouragement and in-fighting among the congregation, and the delivery of a guiding covenant from the mountain top. Underneath all they have endured together, Moses proclaims, there is an abiding source of support, shelter, accompaniment, guidance, and liberation that has never left them. Everything is undergirded by "the everlasting arms"—an all-embracing love. Keep this faith! Moses implored. And the old Universalists did.

Religion that finds its spiritual foundation in an all-embracing love does not arise from a singular lightning strike of revelation. Nor is it simply dictated by a sacred text. Such faith emerges slowly through a community of people who have shared a history of struggle and hope, who have resisted oppression, endured conflict and discouragement, and found blessings in the midst of it all. It matures over time into a resonant confidence that may only be strongly felt by a few, but echoes in the hearts of others who are within its reach. It gains strength in story and song, in rituals of remembrance and life-passages marked with blessings, in times of quiet communion and enduring friendships, and in public declarations of purpose and hope.

"Love is the power that holds us together," the gathered assembly of Unitarian Universalists affirmed by vote of the body in June 2023, "and is at the center of our shared values." "Amen!" I can hear the old Universalists saying. The journey to this historic moment has been generations long. It marks, I hope, a tipping point in our denomination's "Journey toward Wholeness." What will it take, Unitarian Universalists have asked, for this religious movement to truly be a "Beloved Community" in the context of white America's faithless and tragic abuse of Indigenous people, its legacy of enslavement of Black people, and its prejudicial treatment of people of Asian and Latinx cultures? This journey has been one of hope and conviction, but it has also been filled with conflict, discouragement, infighting, failure, repeated harms, and heartbreak. But underneath it all, something has sustained the aspiration. Perhaps that "something" is within us—an inborn sense of right and wrong, a human genetic encoding for empathy and caring. Perhaps it is among us, a relational bond felt in transporting moments of singing and praying or marching together to confront injustice. Perhaps it is within, among, *and beyond us*, that "transcending mystery and wonder . . . which moves us to a renewal of the spirit." Underneath, the everlasting arms.

The spiritual and ethical challenge of our faith is to stay grounded in this love, together. The Journey Toward Wholeness has shown us this. Not sentimental love, but strong and fierce love. Not polite kindness, but profound respect and willingness to be changed by our relationships with one another. Not mere tolerance of differences, but accountability for the character of our interactions. For all this, we need spiritual practices that strengthen our ability to know ourselves as beloved, to relate to one another as beloveds, and to extend the reach of love in ever widening circles of embrace. As the 2023 General Assembly went on to declare, "We are accountable to one another for doing the work of living our shared values through the spiritual discipline of Love."

The strength to love, Martin Luther King, Jr. said, is what makes Beloved Community possible. Love is a creative activity, a combination of elements that together yields a transformation. Beloved Community is a result—like that childhood project to make a volcano in your kitchen: put soda and vinegar together and "Voila!"—something unexpected happens. But unlike the kitchen volcano, love that foments transformative justice does not happen just once. It recurs in a circular motion, in reciprocity with others.

Beloved Community is created and sustained as a circle in time; manifested in diverse moments and places in which past, present, and future are gathered through love. Love embraces the past through faithful covenant with ancestors. Love looks to the future as people work to build a better world. Love finds immediate realization in the here and now, among those who rejoice in the good that is found, embody compassion and kindness, and engage with what needs to be healed, mourned, or repaired right here, right now.

Tending Ancestral Fires

Like the Sankofa bird, love looks backwards in time to connect with those who have gone before. "They are with us still; they have not melted into the dust," as the beautiful reading by Rev. Kathleen McTigue in *Singing the Living Tradition* says.[1] Love remembers them. Our lives are strengthened and deepened when our spiritual practices include studying their lives and telling their stories with honesty that both respects their wisdom and accepts their limitations. Love does not reduce ancestors to mere valorized heroes who make us proud and feed our ego needs, stripping them of their fully embodied lives, their complexity, their relationships and communities, and their cultural and historical contexts. Nor does it regard previous lives as burdens to leave behind as if time were about escaping the past in an endless march "onwards and upwards" forever, discarding so much that our lives become emaciated rather than liberated. Love, as affirmed in many Indigenous spiritual perspectives, knows the ancestors remain a presence. They are felt in moments of ritual. They speak to us in dreams. They answer prayers with words and insights that come to us when we call on them. They haunt us with their tragic failures that require us to heal and change. They offer us blessings and warnings, affirmations and admonishments. We are in a covenantal relationship with them. "What they dreamed be

[1] Kathleen McTigue, in *Singing the Living Tradition* (Unitarian Universalist Association, 1993), #721.

ours to do,"[2] we sing. Embracing them, time spirals into an ever-deepening circle, flowing like water after a stone falls.

When we tend ancestral fires, we dispel the too-bright light of white supremacy culture, which hides important realities in its penumbra. Beyond the white male canon that over-defines "our story" and the habits of self-congratulation that edit too much out, we discover that the Unitarian and Universalist heritages are more diverse than we have imagined and are not even ours alone. Becoming a multicultural, multiracial Beloved Community is more than a future prospect; it includes re-engaging the past. Those who lived before can become transformative informants who change the meaning of Unitarianism and Universalism now. For example, Dr. Joanne Braxton, in her study of Zora Neal Hurston, identifies the existence of what she names "Organic Universalism," the presence in African American folk traditions, religion, and literature of a radically inclusive and integrative spirit. African American Organic Universalism rejects the notion that God would burn anyone in hell, that any birth is unholy, and that the fate of humans can be separated from the earth and all its creatures. How might Unitarian Universalism change if we understood Universalism as something we are part of rather than something we hold a monopoly on?

Another example: Islamic presence within Unitarianism is coming out of the shadows. Rev. Nayer Taheri, a UU-Muslim chaplain and American literature scholar who came to the U.S. as a queer woman fleeing persecution in Iran, has shown how, in the nineteenth century, Ralph Waldo Emerson filled his work with unacknowledged quotes of the great Muslim poet Hafez. When Emerson wrote, "Within us is the soul of the whole," his immersion in Islamic poetry comes through as he extols "the universal beauty to which every part and particle is equally

---

[2] John Huntley Skrine, "Rank by Rank Again We Stand," *Singing the Living Tradition*, #358.

related, the eternal One . . . when it flows through our affections, it is love." Muslim mystics call God "Beloved" and make Love the sacred center of their spirituality. How lovely and significant that today we hear the use of "Beloved" and "Beloveds" as modes of address for God and one another.

Liberating history and traditions from the constraints of "whiteanity"—the supremacy culture of white, colonizing, patriarchal Christianity—is a work of love. When the ancestors are with us, we receive gifts of deeper understanding, comprehend traumas that we are called to heal, discover spiritual wisdom that stretches our hearts and minds, and experience joy magnified.

Building a Better World: A Calling and a Caution

Love looks to the future as well as to the past. It dreams of Beloved Community in which there is "liberty and justice for all," in which racism has been dismantled, violence has ceased, and earth is flourishing through responsible stewardship. Liberal people of faith can be relied on to work for that future through our determined strength, our righteous hope, and our belief that we can change the world. These are important ethical and spiritual virtues. We celebrate the good work Unitarian Universalists have done and are doing to advance the dream of Beloved Community and we should "keep on keeping on" with courage and commitment. But sometimes when we are exuberantly singing "We'll Build a Land" I am troubled that we also need to remember that our Puritan forebears' ambition to build a better world wasn't enough to keep them from harming the people and the lands they colonized. When Beloved Community is only understood as a future goal that we must make real, there is a risk that we will lose the thread of love. We may become self-righteous judges of everything in the present and the past that does not live up to the ideal and fail to notice and do right by the good that is already here. We can forget our human limitations and our need for one another here and now.

To shore up our own superior identity, we may attack others in our community for their failures. We condemn people who think what we thought yesterday. With terrible irony, our idealism and sense of power can become insidious destroyers of our hopes.

It is important to understand that white supremacy culture is sustained and re-supplied by overactive righteous idealism. Reflecting on the Puritans who crossed the Atlantic to create a new and better world, my co-writer Rita Nakashima Brock noted in *Saving Paradise*,

> To love in this way was always to have your heart, mind, and soul turned elsewhere, perpetually departing the present for something better. . . . to dwell with one foot always in another, better world, not here, not now. . . . Such a sensibility disconnected love from immediate, observant, astute engagement with life.[3]

Our focus on the future does matter. But love requires more.

Participating in Congregational Life

Love must live in the present. Here and now, in covenant with one another, we can practice and learn the ways of love. Now—not some other time—is when we need loving encouragement, mutual care, and respect for our wholeness and dignity, especially given contexts of injustice and hate. Through love's spiritual disciplines we can embody Beloved Community as a present-tense antidote to the systemic evils harming our world; we can provide a haven of resistance to the forces of division, of exploitation, of apathy, and even cruelty alive in the world

[3] Rebecca Ann Parker and Rita Nakashima Brock, *Saving Paradise: How Christianity Traded Love of This World for Crucifixion and Empire* (Beacon, 2008).

today. We can center joy in the exquisite gifts of diverse life, in "this present paradise," where struggle and conflict persist but love abides. We can manifest the spiritual stamina to hold fast to that which is good in the face of opposition and threat, even from members of our own community, and can do so with gentle persistence. We can do more than look to the future; we can bring hope home to today.

We need one another to practice and learn the ways of love. Congregational life provides us a place to cultivate the disciplines of the spirit and the strength to love, including the capacity to face ourselves and others with honesty and humility, to be held accountable, and to know when and how to make amends. Hard lessons come in the daily practice of life together in religious community. On the journey toward wholeness, tragic harms can and do occur, such as when people of color are exhausted by white people undermining their leadership by over-control, surveillance, or unchecked benevolent paternalism; or by projecting unfair expectations on leaders of color and then abandoning them at their first challenge. Hearts are broken by our collective failures to fully manifest what we profess and value.

In our present-tense commitment to being Beloved Community here and now, perfection will elude us. Instead, we need the spiritual discipline of love that stays engaged even when there is failure. Love, indeed, is strong as death. It can and will bear what must be born of difficulty and grief, of tragedy, trauma, and threat. But love also sets limits, it maintains boundaries against destruction. Love says yes to the sacred worth of every person, but it also says no to abuse in relationships and systems. Love is compassionate, open, flexible, and merciful, but it also can be unyielding when necessary to protect the things that matter most. Love cares for others, but also respects and cares for the self. Love makes sacrifices for the sake of a beloved or a great cause, but love does not make sacrifice an absolute, sacred requirement in all times and places. Especially when sacrifice simply serves to protect the interests and privileges of those who have no transcendent loyalty beyond themselves and their power.

Love believes all things. This means that love faces reality, faces what is, and responds to it. It weeps with those who weep and laughs with those who rejoice. Love does not deny the existence of tragedy or the existence of beauty. Love trusts an ever-larger benevolence and opens itself to ever wider vistas like we see on a summer night, out under the stars, when we feel the universe as a quilt stitched with tiny lights wrapping us in a cradle of luminous darkness.

We Rest in This Love

We can lose track of love. Human cruelty can estrange us from it. We can dwell in fear and anger. We can be lost in despair and confusion. We can be cut off from others and isolated in all-consuming self-concern. We can be so hurt that we close off feeling, receiving, or knowing that we are loved, or that life is a good gift.

Spiritual practices can reconnect us to "the everlasting arms," to the great love that holds us all and never lets us go. Music and the arts, communal worship that engages all our senses, supportive small groups that forge trust and mutual care—these can restore and ground our connection to love and heal harms. Prayer and meditation also help. During a difficult period in my own life, I composed a simple breath prayer and set it to music. It stabilized my anguished spirit and helped me become a more whole and loving person. I meditate on this prayer every day. Now after many years, I wake up with this prayer rising and falling with my breath, as if it had been my prayer all through the night:

> There is a Love holding me.
> There is a Love holding all I love.

There is a Love holding all.
I rest in this Love.

This prayer can be meaningful for a group by using "us" and "we" in place of "me" and "I." Though the lines are simple, they cultivate a spiritual deepening, moving out in circles from self, to others, to the widest possible embrace. This Universalist prayer establishes a context in which the journey toward wholeness is possible.

When I meet you and you meet me, we do not meet in a void. We meet within an all-inclusive reality that wills our good and supports the possibility that we can be present to one another in truth, unafraid. This love holds us to account, calling us to do right by one another and not to harm. If harm has happened, or is happening, this Love empowers us to change, to resist injustice, repair injury, forgive, and begin again.

This all-inclusive embrace is new every morning. It is an ever-springing fountain that continually refreshes the possibilities that life can flourish, can heal, can go on toward fullness of joy. There can be moments of illumination, of clear knowing, but mostly arriving at a heart that rests in this love does not happen in an instant. Rather we get there bit by bit, breath by breath, day by day, and generation by generation as we, alone and together, honor the circle of time and keep the faith, through it all, that underneath are the everlasting arms.

27

Love: Our Spiritual Need and Calling

Rev. Jade C. Angelica

Unitarian Universalism is a religious tradition founded on individual freedom of belief and spiritual self-expression. Building on this foundation, individualism, identity, and selfhood have long been the heartbeat of the denomination. In contrast to traditions that impose uniformity of belief onto their followers, Unitarian Universalists have prized rational thought as the hallmark of our actual and authentic selfhood. But over recent years, Unitarian Universalists have gradually come to realize that intellectualism, self-expression, and personal freedom—without love as our guiding light—are hollow, that we need to understand and embrace love as our primary spiritual need and calling.

In 2024, the Unitarian Universalist General Assembly formally adopted a new statement of shared values that puts love at the center, connecting to every other value we cherish. It's possible, even likely, that this adoption of love—which lives in the space between individual selves—has cast doubt, for some, on the denomination's traditional focus on the self as our core value.

During the journey through Alzheimer's disease with my mother, Jeanne, I was given the opportunity to explore new perspectives about the nature of self and the nature of love. Alzheimer's raises existential questions about both self and love as cognitive abilities fade and the ability to recognize loved ones seemingly diminishes. As the disease progresses, individuality and relationships can appear to be fragile. And yet, I found them woven solidly together and gleaming brightly in the tapestry of my mother's life, up until her last breath. Each strengthened by the other.

Consciousness of the True Self

When Auguste D., the first person to be diagnosed with Alzheimer's disease, had her initial meeting with Dr. Alzheimer in 1901, she described the anguish of her condition by saying, "I have lost myself."[1]

Her medical records don't elaborate on what Auguste meant by this declaration, but most likely it was her memory loss and cognitive decline that brought her to the point of wondering about life's most important existential questions: "Who am I? What is my self?"

French philosopher René Descartes pondered these same questions in the seventeenth century, reaching this conclusion: "I think, therefore I am." His conclusion expresses the common definition of *self* as it was understood by dominant European philosophy and theology during Auguste's lifetime, including in Germany, where she lived.

Modern theologian Richard Rohr asserts that Descartes' statement "was probably the lowest point of Western philosophy," arguing that "After a while . . . we think we are our thinking, and this is the hardest thing to disassociate from." And, he continues, "you cannot experience your deepest level of being or consciousness or the true self . . . through your head."[2]

Neuroscientist Antonio Damasio evaluates the logic and persisting impact of Descartes' statement in his book *Descartes' Error: Emotion, Reason, and the Human Brain.* Through his groundbreaking research, Damasio has brought our attention

---

[1] Richard Rohr. *True Self/False Self* (Cincinnati: St. Anthony Messenger Press, 2003), audiocassettes.

[2] Antonio Damasio. *Descartes' Error: Emotion, Reason, and the Human Brain* (New York: Penguin, 2005).

to the valuable role our bodies and emotions play within the processes of brain activity and reason."

During the 1970s, feminist theologians and writers brought forth their understanding of the human self as *relational*. Judith Plaskow and Carol P. Christ wrote that feminist thinkers are "united in their insistence that the self is essentially embodied, passionate, relational, and communal . . . . They affirm that knowledge arises from the body-mind continuum, which includes passions and feelings as well as thinking. They assert that the self cannot exist apart from relationship."[3]

And yet, Descartes' definition of selfhood remains dominant in our twenty-first-century Western culture. In the context of societies like ours, where the self was, and is, considered fundamentally rational, disembodied, and solitary, it's understandable—but heartbreaking—that people with Alzheimer's disease experience their memory loss and other cognitive diminishments as a loss of self.

It has long been my belief that the deepest desire of every person is to give and receive love. I saw my belief manifested in the reality I witnessed, that this desire is not extinguished by Alzheimer's disease. In spite of the inevitable losses that tend to overwhelmingly become the focal point of stories about the Alzheimer's journey, when memory and cognition leave them, people with Alzheimer's still know how to be caring, loving, and kind.

Even as her limitations increased, Mom's desire to give me love was still there, at the very end of the disease, when her home was a care center. In the evenings after dinner, an aide would help Mom stand up from her wheelchair into my waiting arms. Once she was standing, we hugged. With her arms around

[3] Judith Plaskow and Carol P. Christ. "Self in Relation," in *Weaving the Visions: New Patterns in Feminist Spirituality* (New York: HarperCollins, 1989), 173.

me, I can only describe this experience as her holding me like she would never let me go. Sometimes we swayed to music, but mostly we just stood and hugged. With my arms wrapped around her, I could scratch her back. I know Mom loved this, because she always had a broad smile on her face, rested her head on my shoulder, and made purring sounds. At this stage of her disease, Mom's hands were consistently constricted into fist-posture. But while I was scratching her back, I often felt her fingers uncurling—attempting to uncurl—and ever so slightly moving back and forth. She was trying to scratch my back while I scratched hers. She could barely move any part of her body voluntarily, and yet she was making a clear effort to give me the same kind of physical pleasure and comfort I was giving her. Her efforts moved me deeply.

The propensity of people with Alzheimer's to hold and care for baby dolls truly demonstrates their remaining instinct for loving. At first glance, giving dolls to elderly people and others with cognitive decline might appear demeaning. But dolls, teddy bears, and other soft, cuddly creatures can bring them comfort and elicit their compassion. I witnessed this compassion in action one night as I was playing ball at the care center with a group of six women and one baby doll. The doll was sitting on a chair next to Betty. A rogue toss of the colorful beach ball bounced off the doll's head and knocked her onto the floor. Betty reacted to this affront to the doll with horror, glaring at me like I was a murderer. She picked up the doll, cradling her tenderly. She carried the doll to her room, put the doll into her own bed, covered her up, and sat with her until it was bedtime—singing sweetly the whole time.

The souls of people with Alzheimer's—the immortal essence, the reflection of God, the relational potential, the "self"—remain strong and shining throughout their lifespan. Until their last breath, people with Alzheimer's and dementia *are.* Since love and relationship, even more than cognition, define who we are and enliven our beings, I offer this alternative, inclusive, everlasting definition of selfhood: *I long to give and receive love—therefore I am.*

Love That Leaves No One Behind

In the dominant American culture, we most often take our model of love from romance, sometimes forgetting about compassion and kindness altogether. According to theologian Sam Keen, by stressing the desire and excitement of romance rather than "responsibility and care-giving as the central ingredients of love," we create "immense confusion about the relationship between love and care." When this happens, Keen says, "we tend to think of care-giving as a burden that, unfortunately, comes with long-term commitments."[4] Motivated by fear, we could be inclined to avoid that "burden" with rationalizations.

Following a workshop I led at a dementia care conference, a nurse's aide from a memory care facility said to me, "All this talk of person-centered care is well and good. But it doesn't really matter how we treat people with Alzheimer's. They don't know the difference anyway." This is an appalling and inaccurate comment. Putting love at the center of our shared values is one way of saying that person-centered care *always* matters, and acknowledges that because of the ever-existence of the soul-self, people living with Alzheimer's do know the difference! As Alzheimer's expert Stephen Post says, "Caregiving is so fundamental and so basic to human well-being and security that it must be at the core of any acceptable theory of justice or politics." It, therefore, must be the core of Unitarian Universalism as well. Post continues, "Caregivers need an ethic that actually focuses on providing care—on the cultivation of friendships, on noticing expressions of selfhood, on kindness, and on concrete need—that leaves no one behind."[5]

---

[4] Keen, Sam. To *Love and Be Loved* (New York: Bantam, 1999), 115-116.

[5] Stephen G. Post. *Dignity for Deeply Forgetful People: How Caregivers*

In the middle stages of Alzheimer's disease, my mother—who sometimes didn't know who I was at the time—told me, clearly, that she knew the difference between loving care and care that disregarded her.

One afternoon, while Mom was still living at home and I was on vacation visiting her, we were preparing dinner together. I initiated what I thought was an innocent conversation, asking her if she liked her primary care doctor. (We had an appointment to see him in a few days.)

"No, I don't," she vehemently replied.

"Really?" I was surprised by her intensity. "Why not?" I was curious.

"Because he always speaks to the other adult in the room."

Again, I was surprised. This time by her clarity. Mom still knew that she was a person in the room and wanted to be spoken to directly and respectfully by her doctor.

On another day, I missed an opportunity to practice loving-kindness, and I received anger and resistance from Mom. When we met with her neurologist, he suggested that she attend an adult day center in order to maintain her verbal skills through practice and to uplift her emotional state through socialization. After I had arrangements in place to tour the local centers, I told Mom about the plan. She adamantly refused to go, accusing me of coming to Iowa to "garage" her away. Instead of practicing compassion and embracing Mom's fears, I rationally refuted this, explaining that the neurologist thought it would be beneficial. Because I wasn't registering the feelings beneath her words, I kept explaining and trying to convince her this was a good thing. Mom became justifiably frustrated and angry, and she slapped my forearm. Startled and upset, I stopped talking and started to cry. Mom fled the house by the side door and stomped furiously through her backyard. As if restrained by an

Can Meet the Challenge of Alzheimer's Disease (Baltimore: Johns Hopkins University, 2023), 161.

invisible fence, she stopped right at the edge of her yard and looked out over the expanse of the neighboring backyards. She stood there for a long time, seeming bewildered and frightened. Watching her from inside the house, ensuring that she was safe, my heart flooded with compassion. I recognized her diminishing independence and knew just how much she hated that. I realized then that instead of trying to convince Mom to tour the day center, I needed to listen with compassion to her fears about being abandoned.

Years later, I learned from the work of Tom Kitwood and Kathleen Bredin that assertive behavior from a person with Alzheimer's, which is usually in the form of dissent, is a sign of well-being and can be observed even into the later stages of the disease process.[6] Again, we are reminded that the craving for love in the form of care, kindness, and respect is an essential part of being human that continues to define us long past the decline of rational cognition. And when this is not forthcoming, there likely will be protest!

Love Takes Practice

The day of our conflict over touring the day centers, I watched my mother suffer. Through the compassion that welled up in my heart, I learned something about her desire to be heard and taken seriously. And I learned something about the importance of being humble and kind in the context of cognitive decline, about not assuming that I always knew—more clearly than Mom did—what she wanted or was thinking, or what was best for her.

This journey with Mom through Alzheimer's made it crystal clear to me that learning about love is life-long and our compassion can be strengthened. By consciously putting love at

---

[6] Karen Armstrong. *Twelve Steps to a Compassionate Life* (New York: Knopf, 2010), 21-22.

the center of our shared values, strengthening our compassion is exactly what our Unitarian Universalist faith is encouraging us all to do. Chinese Confucian philosopher Mencius encouraged humans in this endeavor long, long ago. Around 300 BCE he challenged his students to cultivate, assiduously, what he called natural "shoots" of compassion, claiming, "It will then acquire a dynamic power of its own."

Karen Armstrong, author of *Twelve Steps To a Compassionate Life*, emphasizes how human beings have always been inclined to cultivate and enhance their natural abilities. Consider the evolution from the protective running and jumping skills of our ancestors to the graceful physical skill of dancers or gymnasts resulting from years of dedicated training. "In this same way," Armstrong says, "those who have persistently trained themselves in the art of compassion manifest new capacities in the human heart and mind" for love, for caring and kindness.

Ancient sages, prophets, and mystics from all religious traditions did not regard compassion as an impossible dream in the context of the difficult circumstances of their lives; nor should we. The phrase *loving-kindness* is well known to anyone familiar with Buddhist practices. However, in the Jewish tradition, acts of loving kindness—*chesed* in Hebrew—also hold special importance, as noted by the author of Micah in 6:8: "And what does the Lord require of you but to do justice, and to love kindness, and to walk humbly with your God?"[7]

The meaning of *chesed* goes beyond charitable giving; it *embodies* the essence of compassion, empathy, and selflessness.[8]

Although Armstrong believes, like Mencius, that compassion is intrinsic in all human beings, she knows that cruelty is as well. She acknowledges, therefore, that each of us

[7] Micah 6:8, *The Holy Bible*, Revised Standard Version.
[8] Colel Chabad, "Acts of Loving-Kindness and the Value of Chesed," colelchabad.org.

needs to work diligently to cultivate and expand our capacity for compassion.

There's no opportunity more powerful for expanding that capacity than coming face-to-face with the diagnosis of a loved one's terminal illness. In the first years after Mom's diagnosis, while I still lived a thousand miles away from her, I expressed my loving-kindness by learning everything I could about Alzheimer's disease. When it became possible for me to relocate from Boston to Iowa, where Mom lived, I then became her advocate and daily companion in the care center. During those last years of Mom's life, I could never have imagined the road ahead of us or how walking with her on this road would change me.

Observed from a perspective that doesn't value loving-kindness, the choices many caregivers make—to move, to change our lives, to go to nursing homes every day and visit loved ones who don't seem to remember us, to value the lives of people with cognitive decline through fierce advocacy—are often met with confusion and criticism. However, devoted Alzheimer's caregivers are resurrecting the sacred understanding of care because we have experienced its relationship to the other elements of love. By consciously cultivating our natural shoots of compassion on the journey through Alzheimer's with our loved ones, we caregivers have realized that the sacrifices demanded of us are making our lives richer with meaning, satisfaction, and expressions of true love, than romance or sentimentality ever could. In a denomination with love as our guiding light, my hope is that all of us will have the chance to experience this sacred understanding of care, both as givers and receivers.

Falling in Love with Love

Although "much of the meaning of our lives is created by tending, meeting, and taking responsibility for the well being of others," Sam Keen warns us that it's easy, and quite common, to ignore or dismiss this idea. "After all," he writes, "news of most any days suggests that what makes the world go round is not love, but fear, greed, competition, cruelty, and the will to power."

Social psychologist Erich Fromm highlighted this reality over fifty years ago in *The Art of Loving*. "In spite of the deep-seated craving for love, almost everything else is considered to be more important than love—success, prestige, money, power—almost all our energy is used for the learning of how to achieve these aims, and almost none to learn the art of loving." [9]

By putting love at the center of our faith communities' shared values, perhaps Unitarian Universalists can come to know ourselves—and express ourselves in the world—primarily as students, practitioners, and teachers of the art of loving!

Early in my training as a spiritual director, words about love commonly attributed to Jesuit Pedro Arrupe guided me. More than twenty years later, they still guide me:

> Nothing is more practical than finding God, that is, than Falling in Love in a quite absolute, final way. What you are in love with, what seizes your imagination, will affect everything. It will decide what will get you out of bed in the morning, what you do with your evenings, how you spend your weekends, what you read, what breaks your heart, and what amazes you with joy and gratitude. Fall in love, stay in love, and it will decide everything.

On my journey through Alzheimer's with my mother, I fell in love with her and every blessed soul living with dementia. And with kindness; I fell in love with kindness. It decided absolutely everything.

[9] Erich Fromm. *The Art of Loving* (New York: Harper Perennial, 2006), 5.

28

Love Is God

Rev. Abhi Janamanchi

As a Hindu Unitarian Universalist of Indian descent, the phrase "Love at the Center" resonates deeply with my cultural and spiritual heritage, particularly through the Tamil saying "Anbē Sivam," which translates to "Love is God." This expression reminds me that the divine is not distant or abstract but intimately present in every act of love, compassion, and justice. It is found in the kindness we offer, the wounds we heal, and the courage we summon in the face of life's struggles. When we declare that "Love is God," we proclaim that love is not merely an emotion or ethical ideal—it is the very essence of existence.

The Philosophy of "Anbē Sivam" in Tamil Culture

In Tamil culture, *Anbē Sivam* originates from the Shaivite tradition, where *Sivam*, another name for Shiva, represents ultimate truth and cosmic consciousness. This philosophy reimagines divinity as accessible and relational, telling us that God is not confined to rituals or distant heavens, but is alive in our relationships and actions. When we love, we touch the divine.

This teaching is vividly illustrated in the Tamil film *Anbē Sivam*. In one poignant scene, a tragic train accident gravely injures a child, throwing two strangers—Nallasivam, a scarred labor activist, and Anbarasu, a young, self-absorbed ad executive—into a moment where compassion becomes their guide. Despite their vastly different worldviews, they unite in their instinct to help.

Anbarasu, who initially seems indifferent, steps up in a moment of humanity. He donates blood and does all he can to save the child. Despite his efforts, the child does not survive, leaving Anbarasu overcome with grief and existential doubt. He questions how a loving God could allow such suffering, expressing the anguish many of us feel when faced with tragedy.

Nallasivam gently responds that God is not a distant being orchestrating events from afar, but is present in every act of love, compassion, and kindness. He explains that God was in Anbarasu's willingness to give of himself, in his selfless act of donating blood, and in the care he extended to a child he had never met.

This moment reframes divinity. It invites us to look for God not in the absence of pain but in the presence of human connection. It reminds us that the divine is not beyond our reach but alive in the selfless actions that affirm our shared humanity.

Love as the Manifestation of the Divine

This philosophy reflects the Hindu concept of *Tat Tvam Asi*—"Thou Art That"—which teaches that the divine exists within all beings and is manifested through our actions. When we love, care, and act with courage, we are not just reflecting the divine; we are embodying it.

Spiritual teacher Eknath Easwaran once wrote, "Love is not an emotion; it is a state of being. It is the deep, quiet, constant glow of the soul, where we are at one with the universe and with all creation." This understanding of love as a state of being guides our spiritual journeys and shapes how we act in the world.

Love at the Center of Unitarian Universalism

Unitarian Universalism, with its emphasis on love as the central guiding force, provides a spiritual home for those who seek to live out values of justice, equity, transformation, pluralism, generosity, and interconnectedness. When we affirm that love is at the center, we embrace our highest calling—to live in a way that honors and reflects divine love. Love guides us in our relationships, actions, and commitments, reminding us that despite our failings, we will make it through because we are not alone.

Rev. Dr. Martin Luther King Jr. spoke of love as a transformative power, saying, "Love is the only force capable of transforming an enemy into a friend." This is not easy love; it is a love that demands action, reconciliation, and courage. It is the love that compels us to build the Beloved Community—a world where all are seen, valued, and embraced.

The Universalist Legacy of Love

Our Universalist ancestors understood this. They proclaimed that God's love is infinite and unconditional, a love that includes everyone and leaves no one behind. Despite facing dangers for living their beliefs, they remained steadfast in their conviction that human hope and courage are grounded in the embrace of infinite, unconditional love. They proclaimed that "Love Works"—not as a distant, abstract concept, but as a lived reality, here on earth.

What convinced our Universalist ancestors was the belief that love is the ultimate force for good in the world. They believed that human hope and courage are ultimately grounded in the embrace of infinite and unconditional love. Four hundred years ago, they proclaimed that when it comes to our ultimate human destiny, "Love Works!" Love works because it is its own reward and its own heaven—not somewhere far away, but right here on earth. They believed then, as we still do now, not in life after death but in love after birth that survives even death.

Love as a Call to Action

Putting love at the center means recognizing that love is the force that guides us in our relationships, our actions, and our commitments. Love is memory and intention. It is the traditions that nourish us and the promise to honor those who have gone before. Love is the bond that keeps us together in hard times and in good times. Love is hope that despite our failings, we will make it through because we are not alone.

Love calls forth our best selves and invites us back, again and again, to attend to our personal pain. In this love, we find a sanctuary where our armor can be pierced by our pain, allowing the softness of the heart to heal us.

Love at the center is the love that will not let us go, let us down, or let us off the hook.

Love at the center is the Spirit of Life and Love to which we often address our prayers, even when we forget to embody it.

Love at the center is the spirit that gently reminds us who we are and what we can be for each other. It guides us to say "no" to unhealthy behavior and to create good boundaries.

Love at the center is the force that overcomes fear, informing and infusing courage so that fear does not destroy us.

Love at the center is loving your neighbor as yourself—not more, not less. It is acknowledging our shared humanity and committing to live it out every day, even when it's hard.

The passing of Article II at the 2024 General Assembly, which placed love at the center of our Unitarian Universalist faith, affirmed these values and our commitment to being a relevant and powerful force for spiritual and moral growth, healing, and transformation.

Choosing Love Every Day

As Unitarian Universalists, we are faced with a choice: love or fear. If we choose love, we must ask ourselves who we are put on this earth to love and how we can embody that love in our daily lives. For me, choosing love means embracing Anbē Sivam and living it out in the context of my Unitarian Universalist faith. It means recognizing that love is the foundation that guides us on our journey together, helping us navigate the complexities of life and the challenges of the world around us.

Choosing love is not always easy. It requires us to confront our fears and prejudices, to step outside our comfort zones, and to engage with the world in ways that are often challenging. But it is through these challenges that we grow, deepen our understanding, and become more fully who we are called to be.

Rev. Victoria Safford speaks to this active engagement with love, saying, "Our mission is to plant ourselves at the gates of Hope—not the prudent gates of Optimism, which are somewhat narrower; not the stalwart, boring gates of Common Sense; not the strident gates of Self-Righteousness, which creak on shrill and angry hinges . . . but a different, sometimes lonely place, the place of truth-telling, about your own soul first of all and its condition, the place of resistance and defiance, the piece of ground from which you see the world both as it is and as it could be, as it will be; the place from which you glimpse not only struggle, but joy in the struggle."[1]

So, let us choose love—in every action, every decision, and every moment of our lives. Let us choose love as the foundation of our faith, as the guiding principle of our lives, and as the force that leads us to a more just and compassionate world. Let us live

[1] Victoria Safford, "The Small Work in the Great Work," in *The Impossible Will Take a Little While: A Citizen's Guide to Hope in a Time of Fear*, edited by Paul Rogat Loeb (Basic Books, 2004).

the truth that Anbē Sivam—Love is God—and build a world that reflects this truth in every way.

29

Beloved

Rev. Victoria Safford

In a gathering of ministers convened I-don't-remember-when and I'm-not-certain-where, breathless from the airport and already feeling out of my depth, disorganized, vaguely fraudulent, and ill-prepared—as usual—I froze when our convenor, warm and smiling, lit the chalice and invited us forward, one by one, for a ritual. Argh! I suddenly remembered! This had been described to us in the meeting's invitation, weeks before. We'd been asked to write a microscopic sermon, one or two short sentences, and share it in the circle as a blessing for our colleagues, and for our Association, which was then (as now, as ever, as always, and by definition) in a time of change and Deep Discernment regarding whence we come, and how and whither.

This convening was about that. The ritual would anchor our discussions. Quiet music began, and I squirmed and fretted in my seat. How had I forgotten this assignment?

For our opening chapel service, please come prepared to share with your colleagues in just a few words: what is it you hope the people will receive on Sunday morning in your congregation's service, whether they are visitors or lifelong members, elders or young children? What for you is the essence of our faith? What gospel are you preaching?

Could it be that I'd "forgotten" because, after all this time, years and years, and torrents of words, I had not yet formed an articulate answer, not yet risked an honest and convincing—to myself—answer?

One by one, my colleagues spoke, movingly, courageously, some in Sunday voices, thoughtful and well-reasoned, some haltingly and tearfully, all generous, all kind. No bluster here, no rhetorical flourishes or arrogant edges, but only grace, amazingly, their words anointing us, the crumpled cards and scribbled slips of paper in their hands placed like offerings upon the altar. There was no pulpit here to hide behind, no robes or stoles to shroud us. One by one, these ministers, old and young, people I'd known and admired so long and many I didn't know, shared blessings from a vulnerability deep inside themselves with integrity that was at once heart-breaking and heartening. They *testified*. The softening silence after each one was like a kind of sacrament. Then and there, decades past my ordination, I was converted, a little, to a Unitarian Universalism I'd not known before, nor trusted could exist. One by one, my colleagues spoke of love.

I've never been an extemporaneous preacher. I really don't know how, nor why, I spoke the words I did when my turn came. Somehow I heard myself telling them, and meaning them, urgently,

You are beloved of God.

(Who was it who said that preachers preach unfailingly the sermon that they themselves most need to hear?)

You are beloved of God.
It is so easy to forget this.
Our calling on this earth is to remember and remind each other,
with every move we make,
every action,
every breath.
Our calling is to remember and remind each other
without ceasing
who we are, and what,
which is beloved.

Something like that. I scribbled it in pen on the palm of my hand, and soon sweated it away.

It was not a sermon I had ever preached before, directly. These were not words I'd ever chosen, having stepped gingerly for years, and perhaps a bit too nimbly, through the theological minefields of congregational semantic life, always skating on the surfaces, not quite diving in. But here, unexpectedly, with the compelling power and the solace, the blessed assurance, of my comrades' benedictions on my head, I realized that for me this is the heart of it, this implicit, inherent "beloved-ness." Behind the silky scrim of woven words each week lay this hope, this intention, this aching aspiration, that whether they "believed in God" or not, and whether or not I did, the people would know themselves beloved, which is to say, worthy, with a place, as the poet says, "in the family of things," a place no more and no less exalted than anyone's place, or the place of the grasses, the trees, the birds of the air and the fish of the sea, a holy, wholly undisputed, rightful place on this, our common ground. To know themselves, to know ourselves, beloved without question, is the place where we begin. And from there, by our actions, by our choices, by our art, by our risks, by our work and tears and prayers and mutual support, by our solidarity and singing (lullabies to children and chanting in the streets), by our tenderness, and when it is required, by our rage--by our love, in other words--to remind each other. This is our calling in this world.

I care, a great deal, about the precision of language, and theological speech in particular. I know the lethal and life-giving potency of words and the ease with which sloppily chosen words may be weaponized or just misunderstood, and yet . . . . I don't want precision or theology or semantics to get in the way of this conviction, this hunch, this simple, somewhat radical (to the very root) claim about love. As music and dancing, paintings, poems, and prayers insist, metaphor speaks sometimes with more fluency, more light, more prophetic possibility, and more pastoral tenderness, than the deadening thud of literal, prosaic explanations. I've not been a minister long enough, I've not been a person long enough, to know much about God at all. But I believe we are called to move through our days as if we are beloved of God, as if we all belong, we ourselves and everyone else, and every living thing. When I say, "You are beloved of God," I mean you are beloved OF COURSE. You just are.

Now and here, in this unlikely, perhaps un-replicated, gorgeous world, this shimmering, sorrowing world, we exist, together. No scientist, no sorcerer, no sacred text can ever fully tell us why or how it's happened, this existence—whether we ask our whole lives long in the idiom of astrophysics or a child's bedazzled wonder. We are here now, and we all belong. Beloved. And therefore my work, however imperfect at the end of each day, my work and my joy is to strive to act accordingly, as if in your presence (whoever you are, wherever on this earth you are), I am in the presence of the holy. I have no other words to describe it, this love that guides us, calls us, heals us, and holds us in its hands.

For Further Reading

adrienne maree brown, *Pleasure Activism: The Politics of Feeling Good* (2019)

James Cone, "Invocation: God Is Love," youtube.com

bell hooks, *All About Love: New Visions* (2000)

bell hooks, *Salvation: Black People and Love* (2001)

Valarie Kaur, *See No Stranger: A Memoir and Manifesto of Revolutionary Love* (2020)

Jacqui Lewis, *Fierce Love: A Bold Path to Ferocious Courage and Rule-Breaking Kindness* (2021)

Henri J.M. Nouwen, *Life of the Beloved: Spiritual Living in a Secular World* (1992)

Erich Fromme, *The Art of Loving: An Enquiry into the Nature of Love* (1956)

Sharon Welch, *A Feminist Ethic of Risk*, revised edition (2000)

About the Contributors

Rev. Jade C. Angelica (she/her) is a community minister offering spiritual direction and dementia care education. She holds a master of divinity degree from Harvard Divinity School, a certificate from the Shalem Institute Spiritual Guidance Program, and a doctor of ministry degree in Faith, Health, and Spirituality from Andover Newton Theological School. She is the author of *Where Two Worlds Touch: The Spirit and Science of Alzheimer's Caregiving*, published by Skinner House in 2024. In addition, her articles have appeared in *The Journal of Pastoral Care & Counseling, Presence, The World, The National Catholic Reporter, The Huffington Post, Alzheimer's & Dementia,* and *The Journal of Religion, Spirituality & Aging.*

Rev. Marco Belletini (he/him) is the Minister Emeritus at First Unitarian Universalist Church of Columbus, Ohio, after serving there for seventeen years. He also served for eighteen years at Starr King Church in Hayward, California, and for two years as an interim assistant minister in San Francisco. He was Chair of the UUA Hymnbook Resources Commission from 1986 to 1993 and has taught Worship, Rituals, and the Gospels at seminaries. Skinner House has published two of his books, *Sonata for Voice and Silence* and a book on grief, *Nothing Gold Can Stay.*

Rev. Nathan Detering (he/him) serves as the Senior Minister of the Unitarian Universalist Area Church at First Parish in Sherborn, Massachusetts, a position he has held since 2003. His book *Why Can't I Fix It? The Questions We Ask When We Love Someone with Addiction* was recently published by Skinner House Books.

Rev. Natalie Fenimore (she/her) is Lead Minister at the Unitarian Universalist congregation at Shelter Rock in

Manhasset, New York. She is a former president of the Liberal Religious Educators Association and is vice president of the Starr King School for the Ministry Board of Trustees. She is author of the curriculum *Pride of Place: Affirming an African American Unitarian Universalist Identity*, co-author with Gabrielle Farrell and Jenice View of the UUA Tapestry of Faith curriculum *Windows and Mirrors*, an author of Unitarian Universalist Association Renaissance Modules, and a contributor to a number of anthologies from Skinner House Books. She was also a member of the UUA's Commission on Institutional Change.

Rev. Susan Frederick-Gray (she/her) was the ninth President of the Unitarian Universalist Association. She was elected in June 2017 to a six-year term after serving congregations in Arizona, Ohio, and Tennessee. After leading the Unitarian Universalist response to Arizona's anti-immigrant laws in 2010, she became lead organizer for the Arizona Immigration Ministry, among her other activism.

Rev. Sierra-Marie Gerfao (she/her) is a queer, disabled, and white lifelong Unitarian Universalist; a longtime religious educator; an ordained minister; and an emerging public theologian in New Haven, Connecticut. Through public action and reflection, she specializes in how beliefs impact actions and actions impact beliefs. With her first draft of her first full book, *Decolonizing: Reflections of a Unitarian Universalist Christian*, she is engaging in an experimental conversational and public editing process.

Connie Goodbread (she/her) serves as HOPE for Us Conflict Engagement Team Director at the Unitarian Universalist Association. She developed a conflict process called Pathfinder; helped develop the Leadership Experience pedagogy and pilot the GIFT program for the UUA's Southern Region; co-authored the UUA pamphlet *Making a Home in Unitarian Universalism*, developed the Small Group Ministry Series *The Smart Church*;

and contributed to *Drive Time Essays*, an audio anthology for lay leaders.

Rev. Ashley Horan (she/her) serves as Vice President for Programs and Ministries at the Unitarian Universalist Association, after more than a decade leading justice-focused UU organizing. In this role, she oversees the UUA'S outward-facing programmatic staff, including the Side With Love/ Organizing Strategy Team, Congregational Life, and Ministries & Faith Development.

Liz James (she/her) is the founder of the UU Hysterical Society and half of *The Cracked Cup* podcast. She is currently working on a book with Skinner House Books. She is an itinerant preacher based out of Saskatchewan, and the founding president of Mirth and Dignity, a UU organization that supports outside-the-box lay and professional ministries.

Rev. Abhi Janamanchi (he/him) serves as the Senior Minister of Cedar Lane Unitarian Universalists in Bethesda, Maryland. A native of India, he is a member of the Brahmo Samaj, a Unitarian-Hindu reform movement that aligns closely with Unitarian Universalism. He is also a co-author of *Katha Sagar, Ocean of Stories: Hindu Wisdom for Every Age,* published by Skinner House Books.

Rev. Nancy McDonald Ladd (she/her) is Director of Communications and Public Ministry for the Unitarian Universalist Association. She was previously Senior Minister of the River Road Unitarian Universalist Congregation in Bethesda, Maryland. She is a national leader in broad-based community organizing and has served on the adjunct faculty at Meadville Lombard Theological School. She is the author of *After the Good News: Progressive Faith Beyond Optimism* and co-editor of *Seeds of a New Way: Nurturing Authentic and Diverse Religious Leadership,* both published by Skinner House Books.

Rev. Jason Lydon (he/him) serves as Minister at the Second Unitarian Church of Chicago. Jason founded the organization Black and Pink, a nationwide abolitionist organization focused on meeting the needs of criminalized LGBTQ people.

Dan McKanan (he/him) is Emerson Senior Lecturer at Harvard Divinity School, where he has taught since 2008. He is the author of six books on religion and social transformation, among them *Prophetic Encounters: Religion and the American Radical Tradition*, published by Beacon Press. He was the lead editor of the two-volume *Documentary History of Unitarian Universalism*, published by Skinner House Books.

Rev. Juniper Meadows (she/her) serves as the Minister of Second Unitarian Church of Omaha. She is a child of the East Tenessee Valley, the land where she found her calling to ministry admidst the music, waters, trees, and wild things of Appalachia. She was brought up in the old time tradition of country music and plays several instruments, including the banjo, guitar, and mandolin. Through her identity as a trans woman, her passion for music, and her love of science, mythology, and the more-than-human world, Rev. Juniper aims to live her ministry as a vocational calling to radical goodness, real kindness, and the magnification of the Love at our center.

Rev. Manish Mishra-Marzetti (he/him) serves as Senior Minister of the First Unitarian Universalist Congregation of Ann Arbor, Michigan. He has served extensively in denominational leadership, including as a member of the Board of Trustees of the Unitarian Universalist Service Committee and the Unitarian Universalist Association, as well as President of Diverse Revolutionary Unitarian Universalist Multicultural Ministries (DRUUMM), our UU Black, Indigenous, People of Color (BIPOC) organization. He is co-editor of *Justice on Earth: People of Faith Working at the Intersections of Race, Class, and the Environment; Conversations with the Sacred: A Collection* *of Prayers*; and *Seeds of a New Way: Nurturing Authentic and Diverse Religious Leadership*, all published by Skinner House Books.

Rev. Mary Katherine Morn (she/her) is the President and Lead Executive Officer at the Unitarian Universalist Service Committee. Previously, she was Director of Stewardship and Development at the UUA for four years, supporting the funding of Unitarian Universalism, including the Promise and the Practice Campaign for Black Lives of Unitarian Universalism (BLUU). She was a congregational minister for twenty-eight years in small, mid-sized, and large UU congregations. She taught student pastors at Vanderbilt and Wesley Seminaries, supervised many interns, and served on the Executive Committee of the Unitarian Universalist Ministers Association.

Rev. Fredric Muir (he/him) is Minister Emeritus of the Unitarian Universalist Church of Annapolis, Maryland. He has served Unitarian Universalism in many ways, including as the Interim Director of International Programs at the Unitarian Universalist Association and Interim Executive Director of the UU Partner Church Council. He has authored or edited five books and is currently completing the story of Unitarian and Universalist leadership and participation in the conquest, occupation, and colonization of Hawai'i and the Philippines (1893–1946), entitled *Benevolent Intentions: Decolonizing the Religious Liberal Imperial Mind, An American Story.*

Rev. Elizabeth Nguyen (she/her) is a Unitarian Universalist community minister and a migrant justice organizer with Community Justice Exchange. She has helped to start multiple communities of justice and spirit. Recent essays of hers on community ministry and social justice have been published by Skinner House.

Rev. Rebecca Ann Parker (she/her) is President Emerita and Professor of Theology Emerita of Starr King School for the Ministry and Co-founder of The Braxton Institute for Sustainability, Resiliency, and Joy. An ordained United Methodist minister, she holds dual fellowship with the Unitarian Universalist Association and recently served on the ministerial staff of All Souls Unitarian in Washington, DC. Her books include *Proverbs of Ashes* and *Saving Paradise* (both with Rita Nakashima Brock), *Blessing the World*, and *A House for Hope* (with John Buehrens).

Rev. Sheri Prud'homme (she/her) is core faculty at Starr King School for the Ministry and an ordained minister of religious education. Her doctoral dissertation focused on Rev. Thomas Starr King's use of Yosemite as sacred text. She has published articles related to UU history, theology, and nature. Her first book, *Gather the Spirit: History of the First Unitarian Church of Oakland, 1869–2000*, received the UU History and Heritage Congregational History Prize.

Glen Thomas Rideout shapes Worship Arts at Minneapolis' First Universalist and teaches at Meadville-Lombard. His work weaves advocacy with art, inviting Unitarian Universalism to embrace its full promise. In spaces where tradition meets innovation, his leadership nurtures community and connection, turning gatherings into vibrant tapestries of diverse voices and stories, echoing with the depth of shared humanity.

Rev. Adam Robersmith (he/they) is a UU minister, spiritual director, and scholar who has studied biology, theology, history, human development, and the arts. He serves the Universalist Church of West Hartford, Connecticut, as their Senior Minister. His writing appears in *Justice on Earth* and *The Through Line*, available from Skinner House, and in *Trilithon*, the Journal of the Ancient Order of Druids in America.

Rev. Victoria Safford (she/her) has served Unitarian Universalist congregations in Massachusetts and Minnesota.

She is the author of *Walking Toward Morning: Meditations*, published by Skinner House Books.

Rev. Shige Sakurai (they/them) serves as a senior executive at the Unitarian Universalist Association. They are also an adjunct professor at American University and an Editorial Board member for the *Including Disability* journal. They founded International Pronouns Day and authored Pronouns.org. Rev. Sakurai is a Unitarian Universalist with atheist, Shinto, Buddhist, and Christian heritages, ordained in a nature spirituality Druid tradition.

Rev. Bill Sinkford (he/him) served as the seventh President of the Unitarian Universalist Association, and the first Black President of a traditionally white denomination, from 2001 to 2009. He also served as one of three Interim UUA Co-Presidents in 2017. He is Minister Emeritus of the First Unitarian Church of Portland, Oregon, and recently completed service as Transitional Minister at All Souls Church Unitarian in Washington, DC.

Rev. Mykal O. Slack (he/him), minister, musician, facilitator, and writer, serves as the Community Minister for Worship and Spiritual Care and sits on the Organizing Collective Board of Directors for Black Lives of Unitarian Universalism (BLUU). BLUU is an organization and spiritual community that provides support, care, and resources for Black UUs and Black people who share our UU values. He is also a co-founder of the Transforming Hearts Collective, a group whose focus is on spiritual resilience for LGBTQ+ people, as well as resourcing congregations and organizations for the work of radical welcome and culture shift.

Robert C. Spirko (he/him) is Co-chair of the Article II Study Commission. He has formerly served as Dean of the Southern UU Leadership Experience and on the Southern Region Adjunct Staff Team. He is a lay leader at Foothills Unitarian Universalist Fellowship in Maryville, Tennessee. He works as a Senior Lecturer in English at the University of Tennessee where he teaches courses on disability, poetry, rhetoric, and composition.

Rev. Sam Teitel (he/him) is a Unitarian Universalist minister and poet currently serving as the minister of The Church of the River in Memphis, Tennessee. He has a sermon in *One Nation, Indivisible: Seeking Liberty and Justice from the Pulpit to the Streets*, edited by Celine Ibrahim.

Rev. Karen Van Fossan (she/her) is a Water Protector, abolitionist minister, licensed professional counselor, and author of *A Fire at the Center: Solidarity, Whiteness, and Becoming a Water Protector*, published by Skinner House Books. As Director of Authentic Ministry, she is devoted to collective liberation and spiritual renewal.